First Home

Books by Leslie Linsley

Leslie Linsley's Weekend Decorating
Leslie Linsley's 15-Minute Decorating Ideas
Leslie Linsley's Quick Christmas Decorating Ideas
Nantucket Style
Key West Houses
Hooked Rugs
The Weekend Quilt
A Quilter's Country Christmas
Country Decorating with Fabric Crafts
Christmas Ornaments and Stockings
New Ideas for Old Furniture
Fabulous Furniture Decorations
Découpage: A New Look at an Old Craft
Scrimshaw: A Traditional Folk Art

First Home

A Decorating Guide and Sourcebook for the First Time Around

Leslie Linsley

Illustrations by Jon Aron

Quill
William Morrow
New York

A Nantucket Press Book

Library of Congress Cataloging-in-Publication Data

Linsley, Leslie
    First home: a decorating guide and sourcebook for the first time
        around / Leslie Linsley.
        p. cm.
    "A Nantucket Press book"—T.p. verso.
    Includes index.
    ISBN 0-688-15137-X
    1. Interior decoration—Handbooks, manuals, etc.   I. Title.
NK2115.L578   1998
747—dc21   97-37174
                                                        CIP

Printed in the United States of America

First Paperback Edition

1 2 3 4 5 6 7 8 9 10

BOOK DESIGN BY JON ARON

Contents

First Home

Introduction

When I bought my first home, I remember being both excited and frustrated about how I would fill each room with furniture. I think I chose the house I did because I liked the way the owners had furnished it. Their choice of paint colors and carpeting was stylish and I could imagine living there. I didn't really think much about decorating each and every square inch once they moved out. I was just excited to be owning my own home.

This euphoria was short-lived. When the previous owners moved out and I walked through the empty rooms for the first time, it was painfully apparent that I needed "stuff." What little I owned wouldn't begin to fill the space, and most of it wouldn't fit, or was all wrong. I needed a plan, and a quick one, since I had no intention of devoting all my free time to decorating. With a very limited budget, whatever I bought would have to be the most important items; the "I-can't-live-without-a-bed" items, for example, leaving the accessories or fun things for later.

I realized that the problem of getting a house to look like a home was something I hadn't fully grasped. However, it became an interesting challenge, and I don't think I ever enjoyed furnishing the many homes I've subsequently lived in quite as much as I enjoyed doing the first one.

Decorating your first home can be a bit overwhelming. Most people don't know where to begin. They don't know what they want or need, or how to go about establishing priorities. Few have unlimited resources or the time to devote to creating a satisfying, comfortable environment. Some of your requirements will likely result in spending a considerable amount of money, such as buying a sofa or a dining room table and chairs, so it pays to acquire some basic knowledge and develop some sort of plan, no matter how loose. Many other decisions may cost less, but they are similarly daunting, from making choices that are compatible with the way you live to deciding how to cover floors and windows. I'll bet you never realized how many windows you had until you draped a bath towel over your bedroom window that first night in your first home.

I have a little shop on Nantucket, where we sell handmade home accessories. During the course of the season, I talk to hundreds of people, all looking for things to improve the look of their homes. But very few people know exactly what they want, until they stumble upon something that speaks to them.

Many of my customers are two-career couples who are too busy to decorate, but they want their homes to look stylish. They just want to get the process over with. One couple told me they're tired of eating dinner perched on stools at the kitchen counter and are at the point where almost any table and chairs will do. It's true, at some point you have to make a decision. But if you know your style is formal, at least you won't live to regret the impulsive purchase of a scrubbed-pine dining table and colonial chairs.

Moving In

Don't be in a hurry and don't be embarrassed if your house or apartment is filled with empty space for a while. Take your time. I know this is hard for many people who are used to being organized and getting to end results quickly in other areas of their lives. But if you take the time to get necessary information, you'll be able to figure out what you need and like. In this way you'll be a lot more successful in creating the look and feel that will please you, especially if you don't yet know what that is. You'll save a lot of money, too.

What Is Style?

Style is a combination of the way you live and the way you furnish your home. Bringing the two into accord is the trick and, when done well, will result in a home that is a pleasure to look at and live in. What you end up with is an environment that makes you feel good.

I'm often asked, "What's the current, most popular, decorating style?" Following decorating trends can be dangerous. Styles go in and out of fashion, but what you should strive for is a home that has a timeless look. One shouldn't be able to tell if your home was decorated in the 1930s or the 1990s. Homes furnished with an eclectic mix of carefully selected things are usually the most interesting.

I spoke to several of my friends who are editors at decorating magazines about the future of interior design. All agree that style comes from the ability to combine old and new, traditional and modern, and cost is never a factor. One can be as proud of great farmhouse kitchen chairs found at a yard sale and repainted as of a wonderful Italian chair bought at a New York City auction house. In fact, a careful shopper can always spot a well-designed item at a discount outlet and know how to use it. In the end, what something costs is less important than how great it looks with everything else in the room. What matters is the overall effect.

Whimsy is always appreciated and a sense of humor should be displayed somewhere. The element of surprise gives a room interest. For example, using something in an unexpected way, or hanging a picture where you wouldn't expect it, is one way to introduce this aspect into your home.

When deciding what to buy, you'll be asking yourself if it will add pleasure to your life. If you think it will just collect dust and won't make you happy to look at it, don't buy it. The main theme of decorating for today is carefree, elegant and a little spare. Clutter isn't conducive to today's style of living.

Developing Personal Style

The best way to develop a personal style is to define what you like. This does not mean you have to take a course in Decorating 101. But you do have to do something you've probably already been doing for months now anyway: looking at decorating magazines and style books, going through home-furnishings stores in your spare time, and checking out your friends' homes. And you should do all this before buying one single thing.

Long before you choose your color scheme, your furnishings, or fabrics, you have to decide, however loosely, what your style of living is or will become. Maybe this home is meant to change the way you've always lived in the past. Perhaps you're now moving into another stage of your life, leaving a cramped apartment for the luxury of a first house, with rooms that don't have to serve more than one purpose. Or you may be trading the dormitory lifestyle of your previous space for a more sophisticated way of living.

Most of the decorating books advise you to define your lifestyle before buying one thing. Decorating can also offer an opportunity to reinvent yourself. The house or apartment you're moving into has a personality already, and when you chose it, something about it spoke to you. You could imagine living there. Either it suits your personality and lifestyle, or you imagined what your life could be living in that place. Go with that first feeling and expand on it. This is the basis for developing your style.

Getting Started

Gathering as much visual material as possible is a great way to begin. Nothing arms us for making responsible decisions better than information. The more you know about yourself, what kinds of environments make you feel the most comfortable, and the rooms you're most attracted to, the more successful you'll be at decorating your first home.

Online Help

For anyone who surfs the net, there are a number of Web sites described throughout the book. They all cover decorating or home-furnishings information. Some include or have links to remodeling subjects.

In order to get the most out of online time, look be-

online help
Home Ideas
www.homeideas.com
This site is sponsored by *Today's Homeowner* magazine, which used to be *Home Mechanix* magazine. It is loaded with all kinds of information for homeowners. Hundreds of articles on all areas of home remodeling and improvement are available.

Magazines are a great source of up-to-date information on all aspects of home furnishings and design. Get familiar with the publications that have an approach to style that appeals to you.

American Homestyle
Architectural Digest
Better Homes & Gardens
Country Home
Country Living
Elle Decor
Family Circle
Family Handyman
Good Housekeeping
Home
House Beautiful
Ladies' Home Journal
McCall's
Martha Stewart Living
Metropolitan Home
Redbook
Southern Living
Today's Homeowner
Traditional Home
Victoria
Woman's Day
Woman's World

online help
The Homearts Network
www.homearts.com
This site includes the home pages for online versions of *Country Living, Good Housekeeping, Redbook, Popular Mechanics, House Beautiful* and others.

yond the home page and check out all the links that might be of interest to you. You may find some surprises. The Web site listed in the sidebar (www.homearts.com) belongs to the Hearst Corporation. It features material from *Country Living, Good Housekeeping, Redbook* and *Popular Mechanics* magazines. For decorating ideas, you'll find something in each area that may be of interest to you.

Click on *Country Living* and, among many other choices, there is the link to "Collecting, What's Hot and What's Not."

Good Housekeeping is a good source for instant consumer ratings via their GH Institute, offering extensive descriptions, testing results, and recommendations on a variety of home related products

Popular Mechanics has a link that answers all your questions about appliance care, from how to maintain a dehumidifier to replacing a refrigerator door gasket.

Redbook has "Heloise's Helpline" for all those household tips, as well as the antique and collectible experts Ralph and Terry Kovel, who tell you all about collectibles.

There are links to High Point, the furniture center in North Carolina, where magazine editors give their rundowns on the new furniture trends.

"Ask Peggy" is an interactive site where you can ask questions. *House Beautiful* editor Margaret Kennedy answers them in her column.

Books

There is an endless variety of full color, lavish picture books on different decorating styles that are excellent for reference, such as *English Style, French Country Style, Caribbean Style, Italian Style, Japanese Style* and *Scandinavian Style*. There are books devoted to styles such as Shaker, American country, Southwestern and Victorian. They offer tremendous inspiration for furnishing your own home. I often photocopy pages with details I want to remember, and I keep them in my folder.

Making a Plan

Start your first home-decorating project with a blank notebook. Your notebook should also have a pocket on the front or back cover for holding samples of fabric, wallpaper or paint color chips you'll collect further along. A loose-leaf notebook is good because you can have divider pages with tabs identifying each room of your home. You can also add pages to sections where more are needed.

Fill the first section with notes related to defining your style. Then divide the notebook into sections with a heading for each room in your home. There might also be a heading for outdoor living as well as reference and resource material. Leave several sections blank for "Accessories," "Things I Own," "Do-It-Yourself Projects" and a list of service people such as upholsterers, electricians and carpet layers, as well as stores.

In the first section, write down your likes and dislikes. For example, are you more comfortable when your surroundings are sparse, or do you like the comfort of things, such as knickknacks on tables and lots of furniture? Do you like rooms that are monochromatic or colorful? What colors are your favorites? Do you like light woods, or are you more attracted to dark mahogany furniture, for example? Do you like windows that are heavily draped or do you prefer the sparser look of blinds?

You don't have to label your style, such as traditional or country or minimalism, because there are so many different looks within these styles. You may, for example, find a table that you adore. What difference does it make if it's a specific style, perhaps different from the style of sofa you chose? In fact, eclectic style is becoming increasingly popular because it combines a variety of styles and periods and allows for more flexible choices. It is also easier to create a more interesting and personal look. And too, more and more young people are opting to decorate with family heirlooms because it gives them a feeling of continuity. This is quite different from recycling an old sofa bed and requires selectivity.

Some things on your list don't have to relate to decorating likes and dislikes. They might be related to how you live. What's your favorite way to entertain? A sit-down dinner in a dining room or a casual gathering for supper in the kitchen?

Eventually, you'll be able to select the furnishings that will allow you to live that way as seamlessly as possible. If you have children and your everyday life is casual, you might also want to allow for the fact that occasionally you like to have a formal, sit down dinner at a beautifully set table in a gracious environment. In this case, your choice of furnishings and decorating style should accommodate a variety of needs.

Using What You Have

Most of us already have some furnishings from a past life and have mixed emotions about them. Either we feel lucky to be starting with something, or wish we could start from scratch. But most people can't imagine getting rid of a perfectly good sofa bed. This is something you'll have to solve with your conscience and pocketbook. If you can justify getting rid of the things you don't want to drag with you, do so. If not, find an acceptable way to use them. Don't think this means resigning yourself to a still usable chair that you hate. Some things have the potential for a redo and many such items have turned out to be rather interesting pieces. Look at everything you have with this in mind.

For example, I had a large Berber carpet that was too dull-looking in my living room. I had it cleaned, cut down and rebound for use in a den. Most of the furniture covers it, and it just fades into the background. I ended up with an affordable floor covering in the den, long before I thought I'd have the money allocated for this item, which was a very low priority on my list.

On the other hand, a friend of mine who is a bachelor just moved into his first apartment, one side of a duplex house. It is tiny and has no distinguishing characteristics. The first floor consists of one large open room that contains the kitchen, dining area and living room. He loves antiques, but the apartment came furnished with, among other things, a very large, Danish modern bookcase/storage unit. He convinced his landlord to remove most of the furniture so the bookcase could be positioned in such a way as to become a divider between the living room and kitchen/eating areas. Serving as a half wall, it stores all the knickknacks and interesting accessories he collects, along with an eclectic assortment of books. The top is filled to the ceiling with a collection of old bottles interspersed with hanging ivy plants. The rest of the space is decorated with wonderful antique furniture and the kitchen isn't in constant view. Since he loves to cook and have dinner parties, the use of the large piece of undesirable furniture became an asset.

I Have, I Need

Make a page heading in your notebook called "What I Have" and another called "What I Need." Then list the things you have, followed by a list of the things you need.

Carefully review the things you have, and assign rooms in which they will be placed. Note whether they need transforming before becoming acceptable. For example, if you have a sofa, determine whether or not you can use it as is, or if it will present a problem because everything must revolve around it. Can it be slipcovered? Do this with all the things you own. Assess the value of using each item. Decide if it's a great piece and you can build a room around it, if it's passable enough to make it work, or if you can afford to get rid of it. Keep in mind that some items can be used for purposes other than originally intended. For example, my bachelor friend inherited two small, square commodes made of beautiful cherry wood. He needed a coffee table, and while one commode was too small for this purpose, two placed side by side were perfect and provided more flexibility than one solid piece of furniture.

Indicate which items you will keep for now, but would like to replace at a later time. Assign numbers in descending order for each piece you will replace, when you can afford to do so. Once you've made a master plan, you can refine it by eliminating the least important purchases in order to get the things that mean the most to you. In this way, you're always doing research. When shopping for a sofa, for example, in the back of your mind you know you'll replace the kitchen table next. Keep a casual eye open for this item, without getting into it in earnest. When you actually start to look at tables, you'll be surprised at how much you've unconsciously taken in.

The Budget

I admit I'm not very good when it comes to creating a budget. I generally jump right in, buy the one thing I need most, and then worry about when, or if, I'll ever

If it's possible to paint the rooms in your new home before moving in, do so, even if you haven't chosen the colors. Paint everything white. You can always make the second coat another color, and your new home will seem bright and clean. If you can't paint before moving in, do it before unpacking. Leave everything in the middle of the rooms.

be able to buy anything else. But as a responsible person, I have to advise against what I do or your house will be forever empty.

If possible, begin by listing absolutely everything you'd like to have in every room, regardless of cost. List the things you intend to make over and write down how much time you think it will take to do each project. Then list what you need right away, what can wait, and guesstimate how long you think the complete project will take. Next, establish a realistic budget and timetable for each phase of the plan. You may find that the smaller, less expensive items will quickly establish the look and feel you want to achieve, and these will therefore be your first priorities.

Set aside a portion of your budget for the most important, and usually expensive, items. Most people define these as sofa, chairs, table and chairs for eating, a bed and dresser or armoire to hold your clothes, and maybe floor covering. However, you may feel perfectly comfortable living out of cardboard boxes on your bedroom floor for a while and eating at a card table, so that you can afford something else you want more desperately.

A plan is personal and can be flexible. For example, if a sofa is number one on your list and a coffee table is number five, you can switch things around if you find a wonderful coffee table before settling on the perfect sofa. Just keep in mind that you might have to buy the sofa to fit the coffee table rather than the other way around.

Do It Yourself

Painting and wallpapering are two things most people can do themselves, and it will save a great deal of money. In fact, painting is the quickest and cheapest way to

Tip
Paint the ceiling in a neutral room a soft color.

transform a room and give it personality before adding a stick of furniture.

Saving by Sewing

Another do-it-yourself project is sewing. If you can sew a straight line on a sewing machine, you'll be able to make simple curtains, throw pillows, table covers, seat cushions, duvet covers and possibly slipcovers. All of these add real impact to a room, and, if you make them yourself, you have control over the cost, depending on the fabrics you choose. In fact, if you can sew, you can use better fabric than you might be able to afford in a ready- or custom-made item.

Help for Do-It-Yourselfers

The more you can do yourself, the more you'll free up your budget for things you can't make. Even if you feel all thumbs, don't dismiss this idea. More and more manufacturers are addressing homeowners' needs with products that make doing things yourself quite carefree and easy. They provide all sorts of help in the form of 24-hour, toll-free hotlines, Internet numbers for their Web sites, and booklets and pamphlets at point of purchase. Pick up all those freebies at home centers and stick them in the pockets of your notebook.

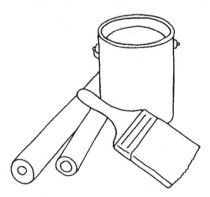

Tip
Choose one fabric that you love and use it to slipcover all the soft furnishings in the room.

online help
HouseNet
www.housenet.com
Housenet is a broad-based information service for home improvement, decorating and gardening. It offers a wealth of advice on projects for the do-it-yourselfer. It also has decorating ideas and tips by Leslie Linsley.

The Floor Plan

Every decorator works with a design layout for each room. Home centers sell room layout kits that include a grid and furniture templates so you lay out furniture in each room and see how everything fits. It's like Colorforms for adults.

Here's how to make your own drawing of a room:

1. Using graph paper of four squares to the inch, make each square equal 1 foot. On this scale a room of 16 x 20 feet would be 4 x 5 inches on your graph paper. Indicate the measurements of each room as well as the height. If possible, buy graph paper to fit your notebook pages, or tape the room drawings into the appropriate sections in your notebook.

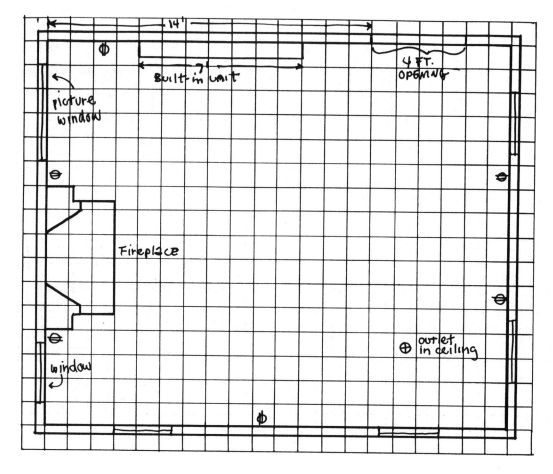

2. Mark the dimensions of each wall (height and width) on the sketch.

3. Indicate windows, doors and fireplaces or other built-ins, and mark their measurements.

4. Indicate electrical and phone outlets, switch plates, chair rails, radiators and light fixtures.

Make copies of your final plans so you can scribble and make notes as much as you want in each room. Staple the plans together or tape them on separate pages in your notebook. Always take your notebook with you whenever you shop. You will quickly realize how valuable it is. All of your measurements and drawings will be used to calculate the amount of paint or wallpaper you'll need, as well as for furniture placement.

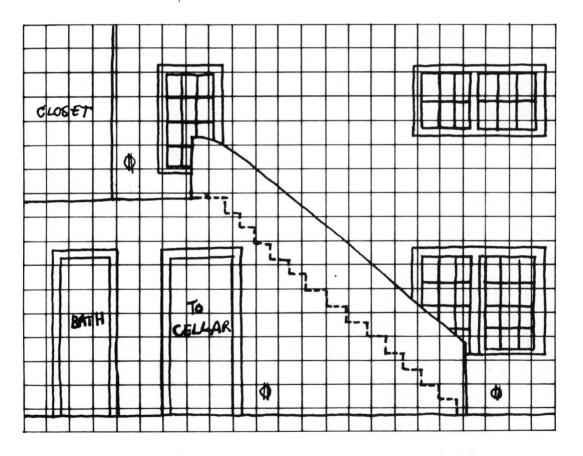

Don't be intimidated by the idea of an entire house plan. (I like to call a plan a rough sketch, which is how I often refer to my house, because it is constantly evolving into what may, someday, be the finished drawing.) A rough sketch allows adding pieces that weren't in the plan. They're the things that you know will add personality or a touch of whimsy when you stumble upon them. There always has to be room for serendipity.

Arranging Furniture

There are several things to keep in mind when thinking through the arrangement of furniture in a room. Remember, we're doing this on paper; therefore, you may draw several different versions of the same room in order to get what you like for now. Once the furniture is actually in the room, you may move things around, but this is a good way to start thinking about what you'll need.

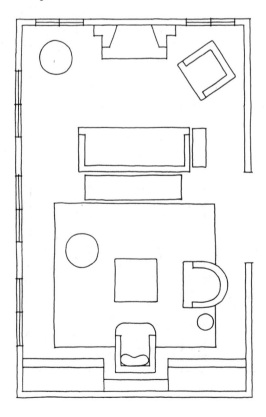
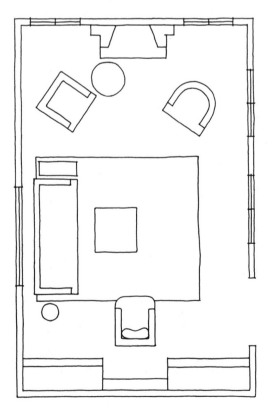

Interior designers advise: Buy something big like an armoire or bookcase. It gives any room a reference point.

Focal Point: You want to find a focal point such as a fireplace or architectural detail around which to make an arrangement of furniture. If a room doesn't have a focal point, you can create one with a great piece of furniture or artwork. The focal point is what draws you into the room.

Anchor: Place the largest piece in position first. It becomes your anchor. For example, in a living room it would be the sofa. In a family room it might be an interesting armoire or bookcase.

Balance: Arrange other pieces in relation to the main piece. Be aware of sizes and how they relate to each other. Then look at your grouping in relation to everything else in the room, and the size of the room itself. Vary the elements by using high and low, heavy and light pieces together.

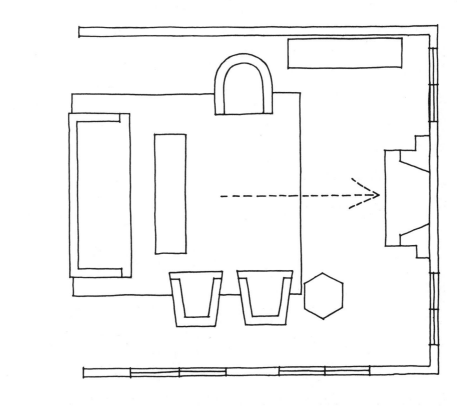

Balance also relates to colors and patterns. For example, two chairs will balance a sofa. They can be placed at either end of a coffee table, next to the sofa or together, with a small table between, facing the sofa.

Traffic Flow: When you've arranged your furniture on paper, imagine how people will walk into and through the rooms. Do you like the flow pattern? If not, you can redirect the activities by shifting a chair, or making two separate conversation areas, for example. Look at the arrangements you've created and try to imagine being in the room, under different circumstances, by yourself, with someone else, with your family and with various other people you might entertain.

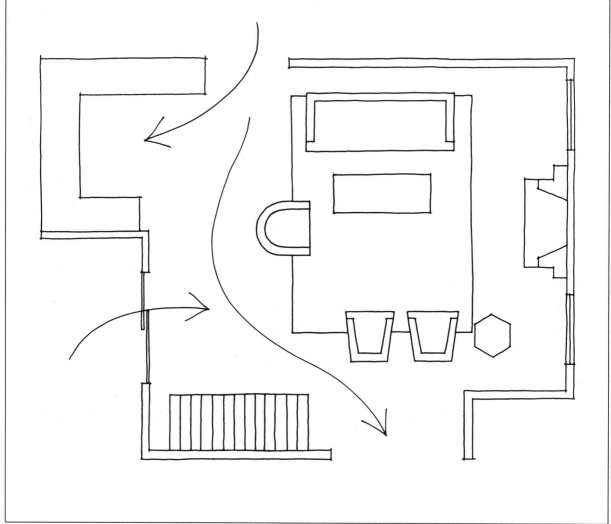

Sometimes an arrangement of furniture doesn't work for all situations. In my living room, for example, I have a few pieces that are light and can be moved around. I rearrange when I have to accommodate more than six people. You might want to consider a flexible arrangement for your way of living.

Variations on the Norm: There is no law written in stone that says you have to have a sofa in a living room. Two love seats opposite each other is my preference. You might have four comfortable chairs arranged around a low table, or a love seat opposite two chairs. Of course, the most common arrangement is a sofa against the longest wall, a coffee table in front of it and

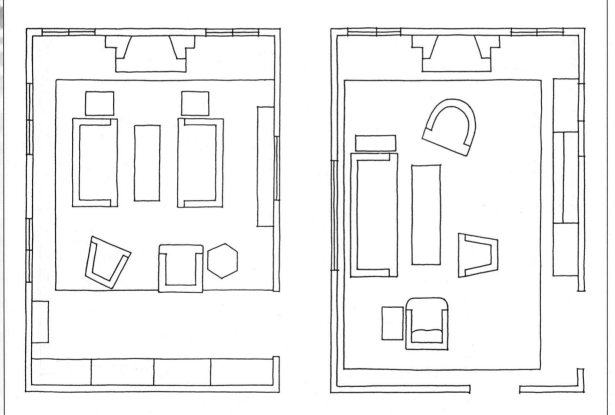

an easy chair at either end of the table. This is the most common because it works well for conversation. You can pull up two more chairs easily, and people can get up and walk around without disturbing each other.

When arranging furniture in a bedroom, draw the bed in different positions. Usually there aren't many options for placing the bed, because of wall space. However, keep in mind that a bed can be placed across a corner of a room or under a window (although many people do not find this acceptable). Before actually putting the bed in position in the room, lie down on the

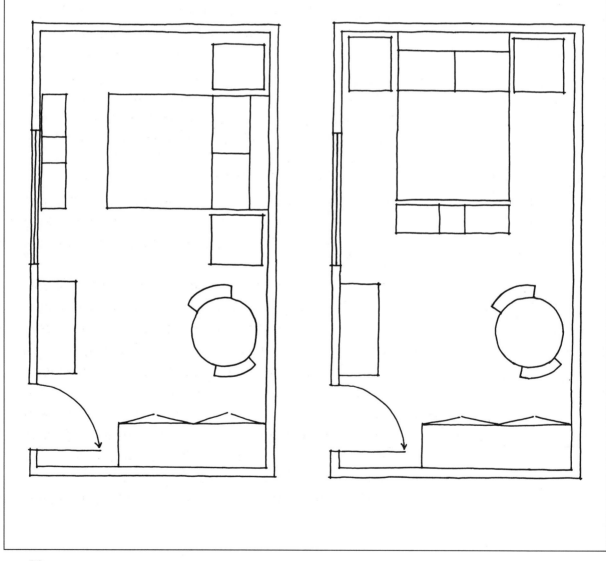

floor where your bed will be to see how it feels. Once the carpeting was laid in our bedroom, and before a stick of furniture was brought in, we did just this, and it was immediately apparent that the bed would be facing the wrong way. We both felt more comfortable with the bed on the opposite wall where we had a much better view out the windows. According to the Eastern philosophy of interior design, the placement of bedroom furniture is crucial to your well-being (more about this on page 124 in the bedroom chapter).

Rules of Thumb: You'll need a lane of about 3 feet for walking through a room without bumping into furniture. You'll need 3 feet to open drawers, and 2 feet on each side of a bed. Place the coffee table between 1 and 2 feet from the sofa. You should have between 2 and 3 feet for pulling dining chairs away from the table. If you want to place a china cabinet or sideboard in a dining room, you should have 3 to 4 feet for passing behind the chairs when people are seated at the table.

Determining Actual Space

Don't be locked into titles. A dining room doesn't have to be used for dining if you need it more for something else. I interchange my dining and living rooms with the seasons.

A young family I know moved into their first home, which had two bedrooms upstairs and a master bedroom downstairs. The kitchen and living rooms were too small to accommodate a dining table large enough for two adults and two children. They desperately needed a place to eat and decided to take one of the upstairs bedrooms for themselves, bought bunk beds for their two daughters, and put the girls together in the second bedroom. They were then able to turn the downstairs bedroom into a dining room.

When we were building our house, the plans called

for a cozy den. Our architect had spent many years designing wooden boats, and we wanted him to design a room that would feel like the space inside a boat. Since we live in a boating community, this seemed logical.

The room, only 9 feet square, has a corner fireplace and built-ins all around, and is just right for two. But before the room was built, we planned floor-to-ceiling bookcases for all the walls, not realizing how little space would be left for furniture. When we saw the space, we quickly changed our thinking. We now have narrow shelves that run around the room above head level, which is more in keeping with the scale of the space.

Don't be put off if a room seems too small or overly spacious; you can always create a design to compensate for any problem. Before planning what furniture you'll need for each room, write down the following questions and answer them as best you can. Try to think of your immediate needs and, if possible, anticipate what you might need in the future.

1. How will the room be used most of the time? For example, the kitchen may not be a high priority on your list because you work all week and put together simple meals. However, if you enjoy cooking on weekends, especially if two of you cook together, the kitchen should be designed accordingly. Even if you only dream of one day spending more time cooking as a hobby, you'll want to plan space to accommodate your collection of cookbooks and cooking untensils.

2. Will the room be used for other purposes from time to time? For example, an eating area for two may have to seat more family members during the holidays, or friends who occasionally drop by.

3. Who will use the room most of the time? If, for example, you're creating a home office in an unused bedroom, this is essentially your room. Since you'll need

to put up the occasional guest, you might select some pieces of furniture that work for both purposes. However, don't sacrifice the functional office aspect of this room for the one time a year when your mother comes to stay for a week.

4. How much seating space will you need when the room is used optimally? A living room, for example, should be as comfortable as you can make it for you and the people you live with. However, you don't want to drag chairs in from the kitchen every time you have company. Small occasional chairs can be worked into the plan for this purpose.

Space to Be Alone

A friend of mine just purchased her first house after living in rented places for many years. The most important thing on her list is a place to be alone in the house. She and her significant other have lived in what she describes as cramped spaces, and she's longing for space where each of them can read, watch television or pursue their individual interests separately. If this is one of your needs, think about it when planning the rooms. Some people don't have the luxury of space, and settle for creating a private corner in a room, with a chaise longue, table and reading lamp. If you bring work home from the office, you might want to plan a space for it, even if it's a desk in the bedroom or a table in part of the living room.

Entertaining

Once you've determined how you'll live in each room, think about entertaining. Do you like to entertain? If so, what's your style? My round dining table is intimate, and the perfect size for six people. My living room seats six comfortably for easy conversation. When I have eight, I'm forced to serve a buffet. In another life I plan to have a dining room large enough to accommodate twelve, but when we built our house, I didn't plan far enough ahead. Ten years ago I couldn't imagine entertaining at all, let alone twelve people!

If your style of entertaining is a casual meal in the kitchen, then make this part of your plan, with table and chairs accordingly. Wherever you entertain, plan to have a piece of furniture with drawers or cupboards to hold everything you need to set a table for company. It might be a sideboard that doubles for holding a buffet, or a china cabinet to hold glasses and dishes, with space below for linens.

Whether you like an intimate dinner, an impromptu gathering, planned meals for several or parties for many, make your entertaining style part of the plan.

The kitchen can be planned with the same forethought. For example, do you cook? How often? Do you cook with someone else or alone? I used to think my kitchen was designed for two cooks until my husband decided to do more than help out. Once he got into real cooking, it became immediately apparent that one of us had to go. I was happy to take my leave. It is now a one-cook kitchen. The better man won.

Creating Ambience

Once you decide how a room will be used, you can create a mood with your choice of furniture, colors, accessories and lighting. For example, a family room might be warm and cozy with just a few overstuffed pieces so there is room for kids to play while parents watch television. You might want a table for crafting and other child-centered activities. Or the room can be light and airy like a sun porch, filled with light wicker furniture and pastel floral fabrics. Accessories might be large

Decorator Thomas O'Brien thinks you should splurge on dinnerware. It's something people don't usually buy for themselves.

potted plants and trees. How you see a room, full or sparse, warm and cozy or light and airy, will dictate decorating choices.

Look through all your tear sheets and style books to get ideas for the ambience you want to create. When you do this, try to look at the details, not the whole picture. It's unlikely that you'll find pictures of rooms identical to yours in size with exactly the same window and door placements, but you may find a corner of a room that's designed in a way that fits your requirements. You may see a color that you like, or a fabric that's perfect. This is how a plan evolves.

The Basics

Don't worry about defining a style for all time. It's possible to change it as you change, without redoing your entire home. However, changing the accessories is a lot easier, and less costly, than changing the basic furnishings, such as sofas and chairs. If you think of these as the only things you have to get right from the start, it makes the decorating process a bit more manageable. Once you've purchased a sofa, dining table and chairs, and bed and dresser, it is highly unlikely that you will replace them in the near future, even if you move to another home. There are simply too many other things you'll find you need, especially if your second move is to larger digs. The point being, don't buy anything you don't really like with the idea that you'll replace it when you can afford something better. I'm not saying you have to spend a lot to get what you truly love. I'm just warning you not to accept a hand-me-down maple kitchen table and chairs from a deceased uncle's house just because your cousin gives it to you. Unless, that is, you can imagine stripping it down, repainting it and ending up with a dynamite table and chairs for nothing.

No Plan Is Etched in Stone

Over the past ten years our family has grown and shifted into new phases, which necessitated a change of decorating style. My white winter living room is transformed for summer with rose chintz slipcovers, but the basic good looks of the furniture prevail. I've added country antiques and taken them away when the urge for clean and minimal has struck. I've gone back and forth between covered and uncovered windows in many guises, from draped to shaded, depending on my mood. I've had a fully carpeted floor in my living room, and now bare wood floors sport only area Orientals. If you get the basics right you'll be happy with your home and creative within your plan.

The Order of Things

Few first-time homeowners have the luxury of furnishing an entire home, down to the last detail, before moving in. More typical are those who furnish each room with the basic pieces, then little by little fill in with what they need. However, there are those who prefer to furnish one room completely before tackling another.

However you decide to do it, you'll still purchase one piece at a time, and looking at furniture can be overwhelming. You have to work at staying focused. You may start out looking for a sofa, suddenly see end tables that look interesting, then go off looking at complete room setups. Before you know it, you've used up your sofa energy and you're no further along. Given the fact that most of us don't have unlimited time, you must try to stick with your original intent.

Starting with Your Favorite Room

When my daughter and her husband moved into their first home, they couldn't imagine planning the furniture for the entire house at once and thought it would be logical to start with the living room. "Where do you spend the most time?" I asked her. And "What room do you want to be the most comfortable?"

It turned out that the bedroom was the room she really wanted to complete down to the last detail. She owned a sofa from her old apartment, and although it wasn't right for their new house, she felt she could live with it until the bedroom was finished. They splurged on a cherry sleigh bed, top-of-the-line mattress set, down pillows and comforter, wall-to-wall carpeting and custom-made valances and blinds for the windows. Since the closets had built-in drawers, they could forgo a dresser for the time being and bought night tables and lamps instead. The room needs more to make it comfortable, but she started with quality pieces and the monochromatic colors make it feel warm and cozy. It looks elegant. She achieved her goal, and they love spending time in that room.

Since the initial go-around, she's added an antique framed mirror and a few original paintings, as well as an interesting handcrafted glass-and-wrought-iron dressing table. This piece wouldn't normally seem right for a room with a cherry-wood bed and tapestry valances, but it works. It's not an item that was in the original plan, but again, it's important to stay flexible.

If you like the idea of one room at a time, the bonus is that once that room is complete, it becomes a comfort zone while everything else is in a state of becoming.

Want Versus Need

When I was working on a book about hooked rugs, we photographed a wonderful collection in a New York City brownstone. The couple who owned the house had two small children and were quite knowledgeable about American folk art collectibles. They had recently moved

---

Tip

A two-year decorating plan is perfect. If you wait longer, you'll never have a finished home. Try to finish one room completely; then move on to the next.

in and had all the rooms painted white. They wanted the things they collected to be the dominant features of the house with no distractions from color or textures. Their rugs were hung as art on the walls, but there was very little in the way of furnishings.

In the course of looking for a sofa and chairs they had stumbled upon an exquisite Shaker desk in perfect condition. It was love at first sight for both of them. They couldn't imagine living without it and knew how rare a find it was. Now they were faced with the prospect of continuing their search for a sofa or spending the allocated money on the desk. They chose the desk, reasoning that they would somehow save the money for a sofa, or forfeit the purchase of other less important items, but they might never have the opportunity to buy this desk again. The desk represented their style and they knew they would have it forever. It would bring them enormous aesthetic and emotional pleasure each time they looked at it, and there wasn't a moment's hesitation about the importance of that decision. In this case practicality played no part in their decorating plan, even though they vowed to practice restraint should they find another such piece before they had a sofa to sit on.

Sometimes it's important to throw caution to the winds and follow your heart. However, if this happens to you, and you live with another person, it helps if both your hearts are in the same place.

A Little at a Time

A young couple bought their first house five years ago. Their approach to furnishing is to do it very slowly. They want to acquire good pieces and would rather live with spare, and in some cases empty, rooms rather than buy "in-between" furniture. Somehow the "not so good," "practical," "cast-offs" and "family donations" are

28

dragged with us for a lifetime. They are trying to avoid this. The other day she called to say she'd found the perfect dining room table but said it may be a long time before she finds the chairs. Another couple I know said they've been working on their living room for three years. It's almost the way they want it.

Making a House a Home

A house doesn't become a home until you've moved things around, removed, added, replaced and actually lived in the space for some time. Since this is your first home, keep this is mind. Most designers strive for a classic look. Subtlety and restraint are more durable than flashiness.

We built our current house ten years ago. It was a three-way collaboration among me, my husband, who is a designer and photographer, and a creative architect. The furnishings evolved and are still evolving, and, as is typical with designers, we are never satisfied. My friends who are artists, designers and interior decorators say their homes are always in flux. It is the process that intrigues us, and we all agree that it's fun to perfect slowly, even over a lifetime. But the good basic bones are there to work with, and practically every morning when I come downstairs and see my living room anew, all bathed in sunlight, I am struck by how "right" it is for us. My basic tendency to be overly critical aside, the house works for the way we live.

Rooms for Living

The late great designer Angelo Donghia once said, "If it's not comfortable, it's in the way." Living rooms are no longer formal affairs cordoned off for entertaining only. Living spaces are shrinking and not many people can afford to keep a main room unused most of the time. Aside from living rooms, we have great rooms, rec rooms, dens and rooms for informal family gathering open to the kitchen.

Living rooms are usually where we put most of our effort and budget when it comes to decorating. It's like putting our best foot forward. When planning this room, if at all possible, try to imagine not only how you'll use this room now, but several years from now. Lifestyles change, and if you can anticipate this, you can make long-term decisions in designing this room.

A young couple in town paid a lot of money for their white silk sofa and chairs, as well as off-white wall-to-wall carpeting. A year later they had a baby and their attitude about decorating changed enormously. "It's not that we would have chosen spit-up green or anything like that," the wife said. "We would have stuck with our monochromatic scheme but chosen more practical, stain-resistant fabrics."

The essentials of designing a comfortable room are color, balance and harmony. If you can make them work together the room will look good and feel good because it reflects your style.

The walls, the ceiling, the floor and the windows are the background for everything else that goes into a room. Once you know what you want to do with them, the rest is easy.

online help
National Decorating Products Association
www.pdra.org
This is an excellent place to get advice on how best to use paint and wallpaper in decorating. Frequently asked questions are answered for you.

Walls

If you don't like the color of the walls in your new home, you have several choices. You can paint, wallpaper, faux finish or panel them. If you love the color that's on your walls, work with it. If you want to start with a fresh new color scheme, painting the room is the easiest and least expensive way to transform it.

Paint

Color is a matter of personal taste. There are certain color combinations such as black and white or monochromes that have proven to be classic because they have endured. However, today more than ever, you have a choice of so many different shades of color that it might be hard to know where to begin.

You can't isolate color. When you choose a color for your main living space, the other rooms will be affected. The colors from one room to the next should live in harmony. If a bright or unusual color appeals to you, for example, perhaps you should use it in a smaller room as an accent, or in the fabrics on accent pieces such as throw pillows.

Using Color for Effect

Color can also be used to alleviate problems in a room. As a rule of thumb, light colors will make small rooms seem larger, dark colors make large rooms seem cozier, and vivid colors brighten a dull room. Color can be used to make ceilings seem higher or lower. Brilliant color can create a focal point, while deep, vibrant color creates drama. Whatever color palette you choose, it can have a powerful effect on your rooms.

Using White for Effect

Did you know that 50 percent of all paint sales in this country are some shade of white? And did you know there are about fifty shades of white on the market today? The reason for painting your walls white is simple. It's safe. Any furnishing, fabric, pattern, wall covering or painting will look good against a shade of white.

Indeed, if you paint your rooms white, you may find it enormously refreshing. Everywhere we go, we are assaulted by color. A monochromatic interior is like an oasis for a restful escape.

White's diversity is what makes it so popular. There's no area in the house that can't be painted a shade of white. White conveys freshness, complements every accent, reflects natural and artificial light and will evoke all sorts of moods, from warm elegance to cool serenity. If you're in a quandry about color, you can't go wrong with a shade of white for your walls, ceilings and trim. Then you'll be free to introduce any color, bold or pastel, to create coordinated rooms.

A Little Daring

If you don't want to play it safe and prefer to add a little drama to your home, you can certainly create a variety of moods with strong dark colors like red, green, blue, black or charcoal gray.

Contrary to popular opinion, a dark room can look larger than it is, because it visually expands the limits. Rich chocolate brown, deep green, charcoal gray, even black, all set an elegant tone. Any colors introduced to a darkly painted room will seem more vivid. Busy prints, colorful art and lively collections do well in a dark room.

A selection of whites
Alabaster
Antique
Atrium
Blossom
Bold
Bone ivory
Champagne
Cumulus
Decorator
Heirloom
Imperial
Ivory
Linen
Marble
Navajo
Oyster
Pearl
Shell
Whisper
Winter cloud

If you are confused by the number of white paint colors, just remember, they will all work; just pick whatever looks good to you.

Decorators often paint the window and door trim and baseboards white, for accent, when walls are painted with a dark color, but even these elements can be painted the same color as the walls for a distinctive look.

When to use dark colors? Dark paint works well in small rooms where you might want to encourage a quiet, reflective mood. If you choose light colors for all other rooms, this one room will stand apart. Painting one room dark makes a statement. It might be that this room is cozier than the others, or has a degree of sophistication that sets it apart from other, more casual rooms. It might be that this room is decorated in a more tailored fashion. Keep in mind, though, that flat paint on dark walls shows every scuff mark. You must use semigloss, glossy paint or a glaze with dark colors. It's tricky to design a room with dark walls, but if drama is what you're after, this could be a worthwhile challenge.

When in Doubt

Since this is your first home, you may be unsure about color. Don't agonize over it. Paint every room a shade of white and get on with the decorating process. Linen white is soft and warm, but I prefer a slightly rosy white. Mixing this color is like making a good martini. The pink is only a trace and the trick is to mix in just that little smidgen of color needed to cut the hospital starkness. Everyone and everything in the room will have a slight glow that is barely perceptible. It's very flattering.

Natural Colors

Many of today's top designers are decorating with colors drawn from nature. It is a color scheme that's restful, sophisticated and elegant. Colors like sandy beige, shell pink, taupe, mossy green and terra-cotta are easy to mix in the form of painted walls and textured fabrics. Bring the outdoors in with the use of the colors in your environment. In this way your indoors and outdoors will coexist and interplay. If you can't bring yourself to go with the white walls I recommended, the next best thing is the palest shade of a natural color like sand or taupe or gray.

In southern climates, the colors used for interior design are often brighter and more vivid, hibiscus pink or orchid purple, for example, to combat the bright sunshine that tends to subdue colors. Pastels such as soft coral, pale lavender and celery green all look great in southern rooms.

Common Sense About Color

As with everything else, take time to select your color scheme. Every paint department offers a selection of color chips for the taking. The colors on these chips will appear brighter and more intense when applied to your walls than they look on the small paper square. It's always best to choose two shades lighter than you think you want, buy a small can of the mixed paint, try it on one wall, let it dry overnight and then decide if it's the right shade for you. This might take a couple of tries, but it's a lot cheaper and less work than making the mistake of buying several gallons and finding it's wrong when the job is finished.

Another idea was offered by one of my readers. She repaints her rooms often and is never quite sure of the desired shade when she changes the color. She suggests buying several large sheets of poster board. Paint each one a different shade of the color in question and hang them on different walls in the room. Live with it this way for two weeks, at the end of which time you'll know which shade is right. You can also do this with different paint colors. I strongly recommend this if you are thinking about an unusual color or if you think you'd like a

Color sets the mood of a room. Designer Richard Lee says, "Colors don't have to match so long as they relate in some way."

red bedroom. The color you choose today may not be so desirable after living with it for two weeks. Better to know beforehand.

Faux Finishes

Faux finishes on walls or floors can transform otherwise uninteresting spaces. Paint techniques are not difficult to master, even for the uninitiated. If you've moved into an old house and the walls aren't perfect, a finish such as sponge glazing, ragging or combing will camouflage the imperfections and provide a textured background. In fact, you can try a faux finish on a section of a wall and, if you don't like it, simply paint right over it.

While it's not difficult to do, it's best to read about how to do it, look at some professionally done rooms and practice a lot before covering all your walls. There is an abundance of material on faux finishing and a brief description of the various finishes to consider beginning on page 219. Research as much as you can before deciding the look you want and then whether or not you want to do it yourself or hire a professional.

Another source for faux finishing information is the free booklets offered in home centers where the materials are sold. Almost every major paint company has a line of decorative finishes and extremely well produced booklets with step-by-step directions, full-color photographs of a variety of finished projects, from walls to furniture, and a list of materials needed. They also offer a toll-free hot line to call if you get into trouble while doing the job. Take advantage of these, pick them up and save them in your notebook for future reference, even if you haven't made a final decision about this.

Stenciling

Stenciling adds the element of hand-painted detailing around a room. Unlike a wallpaper border, for example, when you tire of a stenciled border it's easy to paint right over it. Further, you can customize a stencil design to match a fabric pattern in the room. Stenciled designs are used traditionally to add interest around window frames and doorframes or around a room where the wall and ceiling meet. This is an excellent way to add architectural interest where none exists. A stenciled border also substitutes for a chair rail around a dining room.

Pre-cut stencils come in a multitude of designs. If, for example, you have a turn-of-the-century farmhouse, you can find stencils based on authentic designs of that period. You'll also find contemporary geometric borders, cute country symbols like geese, hearts and teddy bears, traditional florals and every other image imaginable. Stenciling is one of the easiest painting techniques to jump in and do. The directions are pretty basic and there are just a few tips to make it foolproof, see page 221.

Wallpaper

Like faux finishes, wallpaper can also be used to camouflage imperfect walls. But most people use wallpaper to create a mood or add interest. Wallpaper can brighten a dark room, cozy up a big room, make a cool room warmer or unify a room with papered walls and ceiling. Wallpaper borders can also accomplish this. When combined with coordinated borders and fabrics, wallcoverings are a great way to give rooms a dressed and polished look. They infuse a room with pattern, color and texture. Wallcovering makes a room look lived in.

Wallpaper doesn't have to be used on all the walls; you can cover one wall for a dramatic statement or to emphasize that area of the room. I've seen rooms in which only the ceiling has been wallpapered, which makes a very high ceiling seem lower. Personally, I don't care for this treatment. I'd rather see a wide wallpaper border around the top of the walls as one possible solution for this problem.

Deciding to wallpaper is easier than choosing a pattern. Wallcovering stores have hundreds of sample books and will encourage you to take them home. Looking through wallpaper books is fun, because you're exposed to design possibilities that you might never have thought of.

When shopping for wallpaper, take along any other color or fabric swatches you have. If the wallpaper is your first decision, know what colors appeal to you so you can establish a starting point.

Fabric

For me, decorating boils down to fabric. I love going through fabric showrooms and yard-good shops. The colors, the prints, the textures give a room style and

Tip for Wallpapering

If you plan to do the wallpapering yourself, you might want to choose a prepasted wallpaper. It's infinitely easier to put up. An overall repeat pattern is easier to match than a design that must be matched perfectly from one strip to the next to look right. Also, there can be a lot of waste with this type of design.

dictate the feeling you want to convey, whether it's country, contemporary, traditional, formal or informal. Even if you haven't committed to a definite style at this point, finding fabrics you really love and can imagine in the room will lead you in the right direction.

Where do you use fabric? Your upholstered furniture, curtains or drapes, if you decide to have them, and throw pillows. If you've already chosen a sofa and the upholstery fabric, then use the colors in the sofa and build out from there. Pick out the dominant color and use it for your accents. Don't be afraid to mix patterns and textures. For example, if your sofa has a bold print, you might choose a small check or stripe in one of the colors for your occasional chairs and the draperies.

Throw pillows used as accents can be a mix of all the fabric prints you're attracted to that look good on the sofa. This is one of the reasons I suggest a beige textured sofa. You're then free to use other colors and prints in smaller doses wherever and whenever you want.

Shopping Savvy

When shopping for fabric, look for the right material for the item, whether it's curtains and draperies or upholstered furniture. For sheer or lightweight curtains you can use almost any fabric. However, drapery and upholstery material is usually woven to be more substantial and is often sold in wider widths than other off-the-bolt fabrics.

Take home a small cutting or swatch of the fabric samples you like so you can look at them in relation to the room and any furnishings you may already have. Most fabric shops have someone who can help you figure the yardage you need. It's important to get this right so you can buy all of one fabric at one time because sometimes dye lots differ from bolt to bolt. Inspect the com-

Well-known designer of rooms filled with colors and prints, Mario Buatta says, "You should use swatches to create a composition on paper before committing to the final colors and patterns for your furniture and draperies."

plete yardage to be sure there are no defects before paying for it. When calculating cost, remember to include lining fabric for draperies.

Quick Facts About Fabrics

Different materials perform differently. Some are good for one situation and not for another. Fabrics with a loose weave work well for window treatments, and the heavier, tightly woven fabrics are best for upholstered furniture.

1. Cotton is machine washable and therefore easy to care for. It's also inexpensive. However, it wrinkles easily and light colors yellow after being exposed to prolonged sunlight. I favor cotton chintz for curtains and slipcovers because it has a high luster glaze, a little body and looks rich but informal at the same time. It's great for tie-back curtains, jabots and balloon shades. I also like sailcloth, which is a lighter version of canvas. It's sturdy but soft and machine washable. I use white sailcloth for everything, especially slipcovers. It's inexpensive, comes in wide widths, and it always looks good.

2. Wool is sturdy and insulates windows in cold climates. It drapes well and is moderate in cost, but must be dry-cleaned.

3. Linen has a nice texture and is more resistant to sunlight than cotton. Often favored for draperies, it hangs in nice folds. However, it wrinkles easily so it's better for straight draperies or curtains, not for tiebacks, unless you intend to leave them tied back at all times. Linen has "memory," so once the curtain is tied back, the creases remain in this area when the panels are untied. Linen is great for Roman shades.

online help

CarpetMax

www.carpetmax.com

The home page for the national chain of flooring distributors. Here you can find practical information about carpets, area rugs, tile, hardwood, laminate and vinyl flooring.

4. Silk is luxurious. The colors are beautiful but can be ruined by sunlight so it must be lined. Silk drapes nicely, is expensive and must be hand washed or dry-cleaned. This is not a fabric to use if you have small children and want a carefree treatment, or if you're on a budget.

5. Brocade and damask are used for fine upholstery. Brocades were traditionally silk, but are now woven in many fibers. The raised pattern resembles embroidery. Damask is fully reversible and is woven in many weights.

6. Jacquard is a good choice for upholstery. It is a heavy-weight, tightly woven pattern that is often geometric.

7. Ticking is another fabric often used for upholstery and curtains. I like it because it's a heavy-weight natural fiber in an appealing blue and white stripe and it's inexpensive. While it also comes in other color combinations, the blue and white is classic.

Synthetic fibers provide another range of fabrics to choose from. These include rayon, polyester and nylon. Most are fairly inexpensive.

1. Rayon drapes nicely, but fades in sunlight and must be dry-cleaned.

2. Polyester is fairly strong, resists sunlight and wrinkles, won't stretch or shrink, and is machine washable. A good choice if practicality and cost are of major concern.

3. Nylon is also strong, can be machine washed and dried and is inexpensive. This would be a good choice for sheer panels alone or under another treatment, such as tie-backs, panels or a valance.

Tip
Too many patterns in a room will get confusing, each competing for attention.

Floors

How you treat your floors is an aesthetic as well as practical consideration. You can polish, paint, carpet, put down area rugs or lay tiles. The decision is based on the size of the room, how it will be used and the style of the furnishings.

Carpeting

Wall-to-wall carpeting should always be installed by a professional. Wherever you purchase the carpeting, this service is usually included in the cost of the carpet. You will also need an underlay, which may be extra. Ask. Carpeting comes in a variety of colors and textures and the price range is just as varied. As with everything else, quality costs. Some carpets have a stain-resistant coating. This is a good feature to look for.

Sisal carpeting has always been a favorite choice of decorators because it's good-looking and practical, and pretty much blends in with the floor. It's a good natural background for most furnishings, is relatively affordable and comes in different shades, textures and qualities. Basically it has a flat, matlike feel as opposed to carpeting, which is soft and plush.

If you have good hardwood floors, it would be a shame to cover them with wall-to-wall carpeting. Interesting area rugs would be preferable. Area rugs and carpeting soften the look and feel of a room and help absorb sound.

Area Rugs

Area rugs, such as a good Persian, Oriental, kilim, hooked, or needlepoint, can determine the colors you select for furniture and window and wall coverings.

Rugs come in a variety of sizes and patterns, so know exactly where a rug will be used and the area dimensions before shopping.

If you've already chosen a color scheme, take swatches of paint colors, wallpaper and fabrics with you when selecting your floor covering. (For details about types of carpeting and how to shop for them see page 227.)

Stenciling and Faux Finishing Floors

A floor is the perfect canvas on which to apply a painted design. There are many talented professionals who specialize in this area and can transform a plain floor with a checkerboard pattern, faux tile, the look of marble, a stenciled border, or any number of other patterns.

Whitewashed or bleached floors create a soft film of white over sanded floors, reminiscent of those in country cottages. A thin coat of paint is applied, then quickly rubbed off so the wood grain shows through. Several coats of polyurethane protect the finish and give the floor a nice luster. Floors in many century-old houses are in bad condition and are good candidates for a paint treatment. A decorator with such a home on Nantucket Island painted her floors in a light color, then spatter-painted them with several different colors taken from the wallpaper and fabrics in the room.

None of these techniques is difficult to learn, but all require some patience and practice on a small board before you tackle a large area like a floor. If you want to save money and have a good-looking floor treatment, check out the free booklets offered in home centers as well as some books from the library to determine if this is something you might enjoy doing. (See page 219 for painting techniques.)

Windows

"I don't have a single curtain in any house, and I don't think I ever will. I like cornices better than curtains. And I like jabots, which go down the side of a window, and swags," says Martha Stewart. I happen to agree. When it comes to windows, I'm biased toward a minimal approach. However, I also dislike the look of black window panes at night. My compromise is to use plain white panels that are tied back during the day and drawn across the window at night. They blend with the wall color and are quite unobtrusive, but soften the window area.

If you need window coverings for privacy when you first move in, buy cheap plain white roller shades for every window. Then you can take your time planning what you want and where. Either leave the shades where needed, or replace them as you see fit.

Window coverings are referred to in the trade as "treatments." These treatments come in the form of shutters, shades, blinds, curtains, draperies, valances, swags and cornices. They are used to provide privacy, light control and window dressing. They can be simple and tailored or elaborate and adorned with piping, ruffles, braiding, tassels and fringe.

Before thinking about the type of window adornment you'll want in each room, take accurate measurements and enter them in your notebook for each room.

Roller Shades

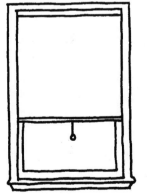

In order to buy the right-size roller shades, measure the width of the window inside the frame. You'll find them in stock sizes at home centers and if they don't have the exact size of your window, they will cut down a slightly larger shade to fit. This is a routine service that won't cost extra. You will find shades in white, linen and colors, as well as those with room-darkening properties to block out light. These are most often used in bedrooms and are slightly more expensive.

An artist friend of mine installed shades at the bottom of his bedroom windows just above the sills. This is called an inverted roller. He attached a small hook at the top of the frame to hold the shade in place when it is pulled up. He needed privacy only to this level and didn't want to obstruct the view of the treetops he saw upon waking. Wanting the clean look of blinds, he chose this solution rather than opting for curtains. This is a good way to gain privacy if you have very low windows.

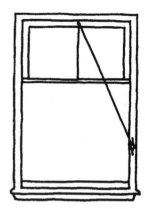

Shutters

Shutters are usually made of wood and are solid or louvered to allow for light and air adjustment. If you have very tall windows, you might need a double set of shutters, one for the top and one for the bottom. Accurate measuring is extremely important so the shutters abut perfectly when they are closed.

Shutters can be painted the same color as the window frame or a color to match the walls. Shutters are often found in old houses and provide good privacy and act as a sound barrier, especially when used on windows that face onto a busy street.

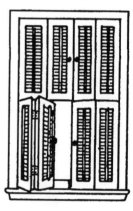

Blinds

Miniblinds are ready made and available in home centers. The blades of the blinds come in two or three different widths and a multitude of colors. They are mounted on the inside of the window frame and provide a sleek look while allowing for the adjustment of light and air.

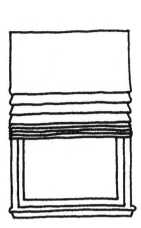

Wooden blinds are the latest decorating trend and they are quite good-looking. You can order these in different widths from very narrow to wide, and in different colors including natural. The tapes that run down the front of each side and hold the blinds in place can be ordered in contrasting colors or to match the blinds. I'm rather partial to this window treatment for looks and practicality.

You'll find accordian blinds in different widths and colors. They are often made of a dust-and-dirt-resistant material and, while they provide privacy, they also allow light to filter through. They also come in room darkening material.

Shades

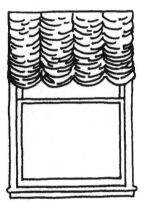

Roman and Austrian shades are made of fabric and operate in a way similar to roller shades in that they can be adjusted by a pull cord into accordian folds. Roman shades are generally flat across and pulled up in crisp folds, while an Austrian shade is fuller and pulls up into scallops of soft folds. These types of shades are usually custom made. Balloon shades have large poufs created by tailored pleats about 10 or 15 inches apart at the top; they create a luxurious full look.

Matchstick Shades

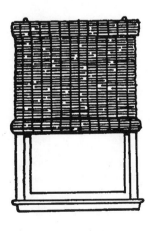

These are inexpensive blinds made of natural materials that pull up by a cord into a roll. They are good for casual areas. Often referred to as slat shades or bamboo shades, they can be made of bamboo slats, natural mesh, sea grass and a variety of other natural fibers. Most natural roll-up shades are not totally private at night. For greater control, these shades are available with backing bonded to the material.

Draperies and Curtains

These terms are used to describe fabric that hangs loosely over an entire window from the top of the window down to the floor or covers an entire wall, including the window. Draperies are usually made of heavy or lined fabric and are used for living rooms, bedrooms and dens.

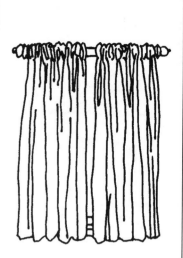

When measuring for draperies, there should be plenty of room on each side of the window to accomodate the fabric when it is pulled back so it won't block out daylight. Draperies can hang to the windowsill or to the floor, or can "puddle" onto the floor for a sumptuous effect. Draperies look best hanging outside the frame rather than set inside the window frame.

Café curtains are often used in kitchens. They usually cover only the bottom half of a window and hang to the sill. A matching valance can be used across the top of the window. Curtains or drapes should be full rather than skimpy. The width should be at least double the measurement of the window.

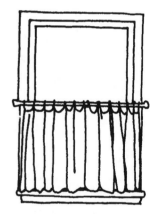

I always tell first-home dwellers to buy inexpensive, plain white curtains, then customize them with ribbon or fabric trim, tie-backs or tassels to go with the colors in the room. This is another expedient and inexpensive solution for covering windows.

Drapery Headings

The top of the drapery that is attached to the rod is called the heading. This area can be pleated, and a special hook is usually inserted between the pleats and then attached to the rod. Drapery headings can also be attached to rings that ride along the rod. Other headings are designed to ride along a track that is attached to the ceiling or inside the top window frame.

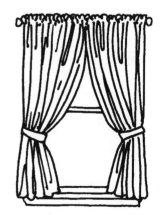

The heading of draperies can be covered by a valance or cornice, which is an L-shaped box that can be painted or covered with fabric to match the draperies. A wooden valance is easy to make and will give your windows a formal custom look.

Hardware

The hardware for holding your window treatments will depend on what type of covering you've chosen. There are standard rods, tension rods, adjustable extension rods, poles and brackets, traverse rods and all sorts of decorative finials that add to the look of your windows. Once you've selected your curtains, drapes, rods, blinds or whatever, you will be able to find exactly what you need to install them.

For a first home, tension rods will enable you to put curtains or draperies up instantly while shopping for the final hardware. These rods are made of steel, often with a white enamel finish, and have a tension spring inside. The ends are covered with rubber suction cups and the rod fits inside the window frame. It is the perfect way to hang curtains instantly without any hardware, tools or exertion.

If you don't want to bother with window treatments right away, you might consider arranging potted flowers on your windowsills if the ledge is deep enough. Window boxes on the outside of the house can be planted with flowers tall enough to be seen from the interior and might be all you need.

Types of Hardware

Once you find the right drapery or curtain treatment for your windows, you'll need the right rods for hanging them. Light curtains such as shirred or cafés are usually hung on single adjustable-width curtain rods, which are stock items in curtain departments. Tension rods don't need any screws or brackets. They simply fit snugly inside the window frame and are good for curtains that you want to hang close to the windowpanes.

Drapery Cranes

When you hang curtains over an area with a glass-paned door, such as a French door, you'll need this type of rod, with a hinged bracket on one end. The other end is free to swing out away from the door.

Traverse Rods

The standard traverse rod is used with pleated drapes that meet in the center and open to either side of the window. A one-way traverse rod is good for corner windows where you want to draw the curtain to one side only. For a double drapery treatment, such as a sheer undercurtain and a heavier drape on the outside, you'll need a double traverse rod. You can also find traverse rods for all sorts of layering treatments such as valance, shirred and drape.

Decorative Traverse Rods

An alternative to using a valance. A decorative traverse rod has rings, brackets and end finials that are mounted so as to be visible above the drapery heading.

Café Rods

These rods come in different diameters as well as lengths and hold café curtain rings. The curtains open manually.

Decorative Rods

These rods are made in a variety of materials such as brass, metal or wood and have decorative finials on each end, providing a nice finish to the top of your windows. The front of the pole or rod is rounded and looks like a café rod, but the back of the rod is flat with slides for inserting the hooks to hang pleated drapes.

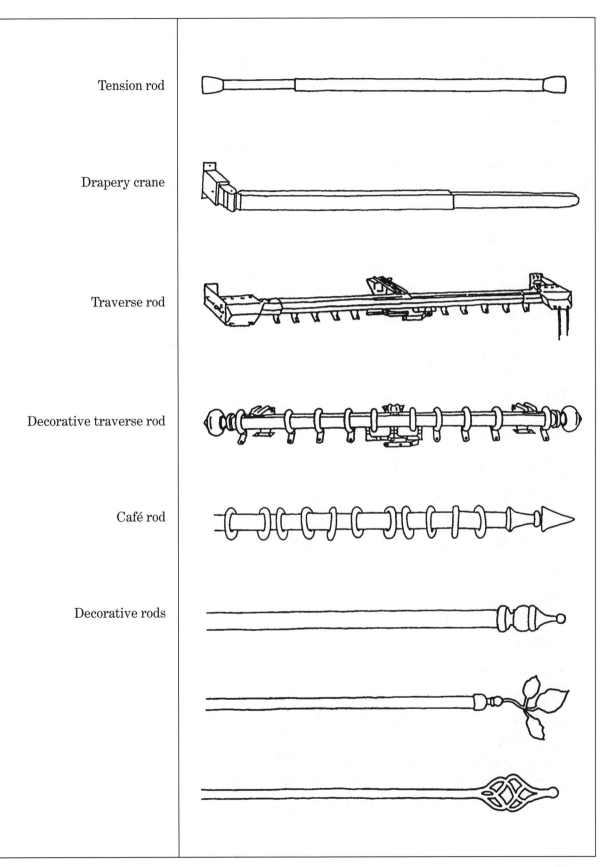

Tension rod

Drapery crane

Traverse rod

Decorative traverse rod

Café rod

Decorative rods

49

Furniture

Fortunately, many home furnishings stores such as Crate & Barrel and Pottery Barn recognize the need for well-designed, stylish furnishings and accessories priced for moderate budgets. Domain and ABC Carpet & Home also recognize the first-home buyer and provide quality furnishings at reasonable prices. They've also scaled their furniture lines to fit into smaller homes and apartments. Furniture stores such as Ethan Allen, Bloomingdale's and Macy's present lifestyle options for those who aren't sure how to put it all together. And designers like Calvin Klein with his Home creations make it possible for you to obtain that certain look you know you're attracted to even if you can't articulate what it is exactly. If you can choose selectively, shopping at these stores is a great way to achieve the perfect environment for your taste.

Accept the Hand-Me-Downs

As a first-home dweller, you might be starting from scratch or with a few pieces of furniture you wish you hadn't accepted from well-meaning relatives. Never be quick to turn down secondhand furniture. Sometimes an old piece may have more sentimental than monetary value and may even surprise you at how up-to-date it can look in a new environment.

Albert Hadley, president of the well-known design firm Parish-Hadley, has lived in the same New York City apartment for more than twenty years. He describes the Victorian love seat he inherited years ago from a great aunt as one of his prized possessions because of its good lines. It occupies a prominent position in the living room. He's undoubtedly reupholstered it

Tip
A little off-balance is better than too symmetrical. Don't think matched pairs.

Do I have it?
Do I need it?
Do I want it?

sofa
easy chair(s)
ottoman
side chair
end tables
coffee table
lamps
unit for TV, VCR, stereo
bookcase
pillows
carpeting or area rugs
window treatment
accessories

once, if not several times, but it proves how good furniture never goes out of style.

If what you inherited happens to be a bunch of mismatched mixing bowls instead of a great breakfront, stain an unfinished piece yourself and give it character by filling the shelves with the old-fashioned bowls. This is how you give a room your personal style.

A friend inherited a wonderful old love seat with a tightly woven caned seat and back. The graceful wood frame was in perfect condition, but there was a large hole in the caning on the lower part of the back. The cost of having it repaired was prohibitive and she almost discarded the piece. Fortunately a friend suggested having a seat cushion made and covered with an exquisite silk fabric, then piling lots of pillows along the back, all of which would hide the hole. Until she can afford to have the hole repaired, this is the perfect solution, and it happens to look terrific against a long wall in her entryway. When possible, look beyond the obvious for creative solutions to make-over problems.

Make a Plan

Before you buy one thing, make a list of the items you think you'll need in your living room. This will include such things as a sofa, love seat or sofa bed if you need extra sleeping room for guests. Other items to consider include: easy chair, occasional chair, ottoman, coffee table, end table, wall storage unit for all your electronic equipment, bookcase and lamps. Make a list of the items you already have or absolutely know you want, such as a piano. This sort of item must be considered in your plan before you bring in one stick of furniture.

Draw the items on your floor plan in your notebook to see how many pieces of furniture you'll actually need and where they might be placed.

Furniture Styles

You can design your home in a distinct style such as country, traditional, contemporary or an eclectic mix. Just because you fall in love with a specific period piece doesn't mean that every purchase thereafter must be confined to this style. Sometimes one great period piece can add interest even if it's out of character with the rest of the furnishings.

When you're looking through books, magazines and showrooms and find yourself attracted to scrubbed country pine, for example, consider what style you might want to live with. Often your surroundings dictate your decorating style. If you live in the country, and enjoy poking around antique shops on the weekends or attending auctions, this may influence your buying pattern.

Sometimes we're influenced by the type of furniture we grew up with. My family collected antiques, and I grew up in a two-hundred-year-old Connecticut farm-

Furniture won't get by on good looks alone. It should be selected for its function, construction and looks. If a chair isn't comfortable and feels wobbly, it doesn't matter how pretty it is.

house. I appreciate old things, and while I now live in a more contemporary home, I have a few antique pieces of furniture and accessories that work well in this environment.

Upholstered Furniture

A living room needs some soft furnishings such as a sofa and chairs for comfort. Tables, desks, storage units and lamps add to the definition and style of a room. In the beginning, try to choose pieces that are versatile and can be moved around for the greatest flexibility.

The upholstered furniture you buy for the living room will probably be more expensive than the rest of your furnishings. Therefore, take the time to buy the best quality you can afford because it will last a very long time. You'll have more alternatives for the other furnishings, as you can often buy accessories for now that you might replace at a later time when you can afford to do so. It's not a good idea to look for bargains where comfort is concerned. Generally, you get what you pay for.

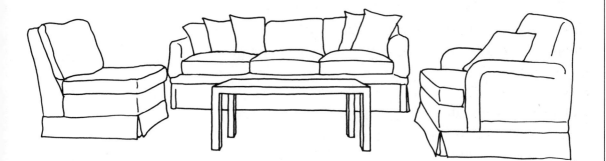

All About Sofas

In many people, the thought of buying a sofa brings on a major anxiety attack. It suggests permanence and being a responsible adult, or is a big pain in the neck as well as a very large expense. It's a good idea to be sure you really need or want a sofa because this isn't something you buy on impulse, and you may make several trips to different showrooms before making a final choice. It is not, as many would believe, an absolute necessity, but it's usually a piece of furniture everyone wants in a living room. Because it's the anchor of a room, it's best to look for one with classic lines. This isn't the place to be trendy.

Upholstery Fabric

Picking out a sofa style is just the beginning. Once you've selected the sofa, you'll be faced with the prospect of having it upholstered in any one of thousands of fabrics. It's enough to unhinge the most informed shopper. The way you see the sofa displayed in the showroom isn't the way you have to live with it. You have lots of options, but you should know that some fabrics can as much as double the cost of the original sofa. Knowing this fact will enable you to edit out those fabrics that will move it out of your price range and concentrate only on those fabrics you can afford. In this way you'll find the project exciting and challenging.

Fabric Colors and Patterns

When it comes to upholstery, it's best to choose a solid color if your sofa will be placed against a wall. This will give you options for paint colors, wallpaper and drapery fabrics. If the sofa is placed out in the room, you can more easily get away with a pattern.

Neutral colors are always the safest and you can add

Take fabric samples home and look at them in the room both during the day and at night. Go back and get others if the first ones don't work out.

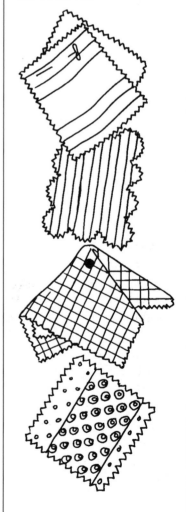

Estimating upholstery fabric

When selecting fabric for your upholstered sofa or chair, it's possible to estimate the yardage needed to cover a piece given its general style and size. When looking through fabric samples, find out what each design costs per yard. Then you can get an idea of how much the finished item will cost.

Sofa: 6–8 yards, full size two seat

Sofa: 8–12 yards, full size three seat

Small club chair: 2–4 yards

Wing chair: 4–5 yards

Ottoman: 2–3 yards

online help

The Furniture Market

www.furnituremarket.com

The site for all sorts of home furnishings. You will find companies such as Ethan Allen, Lexington Furniture, Bassett Furniture and Levolor, with information about their products and where and how to get them. Just print out a picture of what you want, and the ordering information comes with it.

colorful printed throw pillows for accent and excitement. Furthermore, you can change the look of a room more easily when the largest piece is a neutral such as beige, ivory or something in an earth tone. Shades of green are quite popular. This doesn't mean that the fabric has to be plain and dull. Textured fabrics, such as damask or linen, in shades of neutral can be quite interesting.

Take Your Time

Don't hesitate to ask to take fabric samples home with you to see how they will look in the room. While they are only samples, you can see if the color and print will go with the wall or rug colors and any other items you've already decided to put in that room.

Take your time and be as sure as you can about your choices. It will then take about six more weeks from ordering to delivery time. In those weeks you can actually forget what the sofa looks like. I knew a couple who were surprised when their sofa was delivered. They were convinced they had ordered something that looked entirely different. Take time to fall in love. You'll be grateful every time you curl up with a book and a cup of tea, sink back for an afternoon of TV watching, or simply walk through the room and take it all in.

A Little Knowledge Goes a Long Way

With a little background knowledge you'll be able to enter a showroom with confidence, ask intelligent questions and ultimately choose a sofa that will fit in with your lifestyle and the other furnishings in the room. Knowledge will also enable you to buy the very best quality item you can get for the amount you've allocated.

Usually a conservative approach is safest when buying expensive items. A sofa is an investment. You want it to grow by giving you a good return on your money. The return is that you love it more and more every day.

Undoing a Mistake

It's unlikely that after doing your homework and taking the time to select the right sofa, you'll find the colors or pattern are all wrong in the room. However, such a mistake can be rectified with slipcovers. This is an expensive solution. It's better to get it right the first time.

In Praise of Comfort Above All

Every top decorator agrees that a sofa, more than any other piece of furniture, must be comfortable and classic in design. And they stress comfort, even over style. After all, if every time you sit on your sofa and feel the cushions are too hard or it's too deep for gracefully getting up from, or you avoid stretching out on it, then it doesn't matter how beautiful it is.

New York interior designer Mark Hampton knows the key to a good sofa: naps. "I would much rather take a nap downstairs on a big, soft sofa than go upstairs to bed," he says.

Stuffing

What goes inside the sofa is what separates the good from the not so good and the really, really great. I guess it's not so surprising that what a sofa is made of is what determines its comfort as well as its price. Like everything else, good stuff costs.

You might know what a good down pillow feels like. You simply sink into it; it's like floating on a cloud. A sofa is no different. It's simply great. It's also extremely expensive. If you can't afford it, don't feel bad. Down is also very impractical. When you sink into down cushions, they feel wonderful. When you get up, they stay that way—flat as a pancake. A down sofa is too labor intensive for today's living. Who needs all that fluffiness?

Tip
If you want to invest in one really good piece of furniture, make it a down-filled sofa with classic lines. You'll never regret this decision.

My mother has a down sofa that's been in the family for a hundred years. She's had it recovered once or twice and when the cushions are plumped it looks sumptuous and inviting. Once you sink into it, you're lost forever; and when you finally heave yourself out, the cushions look as though they died. In interior design lingo, down has no "memory."

Combining a mix of down with feathers makes a sofa comfy and less expensive. It also returns to "normal" after prolonged seating. A 50/50 down-to-feather ratio is still comfortable and within the range of the average customer.

Other Options

A polyurethane foam wrapped with down and feathers creates a firm but soft feel, and the seat cushions will retain their shape under great pressure. These sofas are much less expensive than those made entirely of down, and some people even prefer them. The foam makes the sofa a little firmer.

An all-foam sofa is inexpensive and will last eight to ten years. It's not as comfortable as some others but it's practical. It's good to know that wherever you look for a sofa, you'll always find a wide selection of all-foam sofas to fit your budget. This might be a good way to go until you can afford a better sofa. You'll certainly get your money's worth and then you can toss it.

Pick Your Style

Most sofas are one variation or another on a few classic models. They are distinguished by these elements: the arms, the back and the cushions.

Roll Arms: A classic roll arm makes any sofa comfortable. It can be low enough to lean against or prop your head against while reading or watching television,

online help

North Carolina Furniture Online
www.ncnet.com/ncnw/furn-onl.html

North Carolina is where most furniture comes from. Visit the High Point Atrium Furniture Mall. The world of furniture is there, with samples of room settings for every room in the house. This site is like a giant catalog of currently available furniture from a myriad of manufacturers. It may be a little hard to navigate, but it's all there to review.

or as high as the back of the sofa. The arms soften the lines of any sofa. The arms' width should be proportionate to the length of the sofa for optimum seating.

High Backs: A sofa with a high back is to many designers a sign of comfort. What is considered high? High enough to feel comfortable when even a tall person leans back. A sofa with high rolled arms and a high back very much represents comfort in the nineties.

Depth: Seating depth is a big consideration. Some decorators feel that the deeper the better. A good-size sofa is about 27 inches deep; 30 inches is considered luxuriously deep, and 24 inches is the minimum. If you choose a very deep sofa, you'll also need good-size throw pillows so you don't drown in it. However, a word of caution: If you select a deep sofa, be sure the room is large enough to handle the scale. A deep sofa will look extra large in a small room. Combining high back and deep seating equals super comfort. If you entertain often, keep in mind that a sofa with deep, soft cushions is not a comfort zone for people in dressy clothes.

Loose Seat Cushions or Not: This is a matter of preference. Some decorators like loose seat cushions and an upholstered back. I like a sofa with loose seat and back cushions because it's relaxed and sexy. Add throw pillows and it becomes a little messy, which can be quite charming as long as the fabric isn't formal. For a loose sofa I like a floral chintz, which gives the sofa a decidedly English sun room look, or white cotton canvas, which is very Italian country.

What It Says

A sofa speaks volumes. If it's stiff and formal, it says one thing. If it's big and plump, it says another. Sometimes the style of a room dictates the type of sofa it

Sofas come in all different styles, materials, colors, fabrics, sizes and shapes. Opposite are illustrations of just a few. Your first visit to a furniture showroom should be one of fact gathering. Make notes in your notebook, take measurements and bring home swatches.

online help
Domain Home Fashions
www.domain-home.com
Domain stores in the Northeast offer an alternative to traditional home-decorating resources. The site features pictures of room settings in different styles for each room in the house. For example, you can select a photo of a country kitchen, or a traditional living room, or other rooms in the house. Every item in the photo is available for purchase, with sizes and prices listed.

should contain. If you've just moved into a house in the countryside, for example, you might consider a casual, relaxed-looking love seat or sofa. For a more formal look, consider a tufted or tailored sofa. A chesterfield leather tufted and rolled-arm sofa and a tuxedo sofa are considered to be clichés among venerable, classic designs and have maintained their position in the "not so comfortable but always reliably stylish" category.

Sleep Sofa or Sectional

The sleep sofa is a good item if you have the right place to put it. You need enough room to open it up and walk around three sides. Most sleep sofas aren't as comfortable as a regular bed or a sofa. They are extremely heavy and therefore difficult to move. With all its faults, a sleep sofa is the perfect space-saving solution if you have an occasional overnight guest and no guest room. Chances are, this purchase will eventually wind up in another room, so don't go overboard pricewise. I would also recommend a neutral fabric so it will work anywhere.

Sectional sofas are not very versatile. Once you plan a room around a sectional sofa, you'll have to leave it this way without much room for creative rearranging. And if a sectional fits your current space, it's unlikely that you'll be able to use it anywhere else should you move. Sectionals have limited use since they take up more room than a sofa and chairs, for example. The sections can be separated, but if you plan to do this there's no point in buying a sectional. Theoretically they're supposed to seat more people. In actuality they don't, because people don't sit in a sectional arrangement for normal conversation. Some designers predict the sectional will make a comeback like most other things, but for now it's more practical for waiting rooms than living rooms.

Important Things to Look For in a Sofa
1. Good quality: This means hardwood construction, hand-tied springs and jute webbing.
2. Upholstery: If there's a skirt on the sofa, it should be sewn on, not stapled. Pleats should be at the corners and the fabric should be of heavy upholstery weight.
3. Proportions: The height, depth and width should all look good as well as feel good. Bounce, stretch, lie down, lean back; then get up, look it over and go through the routine again with someone else sitting or lying next to you.

Basic Questions About Construction

Since the construction of an upholstered chair or sofa is usually hidden, you'll have to ask a few questions when buying.

1. What kind of wood has been used for the frame? The best answer is kiln-dried hardwood.

2. Does the upholstery fabric come with a guarantee? Many furniture showrooms offer a two-year warranty.

3. Is the frame substantial? Look for pieces with corners that are blocked, screwed, glued and double doweled.

4. Do the legs sit firmly and squarely on the floor? Are they made of solid hardwood?

5. Was a layer of burlap stretched over the springs and then tacked to the frame? In quality furniture the tops of the springs are sewn onto the burlap. This may not be easy to uncover, but you can ask.

6. Is the padding stitched to keep it from moving under the fabric?

7. Do heavier springs support the seat, lighter springs support the back? If you want a guarantee that your springs will never sag, ask if the piece of furniture is made with steel bands under each row of springs.

The only other basic piece of furniture that requires this much attention when buying is a mattress. The selection of other pieces of furniture is not quite so crucial, unless they're antiques. Our bodies spend a lot of time, over many years, on sofas and mattresses.

Chairs

What type works where? Wing chairs, wood chairs, large, small, overstuffed or streamlined, they are in a world unto itself. Different types, of course, are better in different rooms and for different situations.

Upholstered Chairs

Upholstered chairs provide the greatest comfort. Upholstered furniture will last a lifetime, so it makes sense to buy quality. The guidelines for buying an upholstered chair are similar to those for buying a sofa. Check the upholstery to see how it is wrapped and covered. Check the depth of the seating and ask what it's made of. If there is a choice of fabric, you might want to ask if it's stain resistant.

Construction

A good hardwood frame is a must for upholstered furniture. The chair should be sturdy with no wobbles. The legs should not be screwed into the frame but rather be part of it. The frame should be reinforced with corner blocks, and joints should be doweled, screwed and glued. Webbing made of tightly woven thick jute is a must. The webbing should also be attached to the frame. The springs should be tied up and down and across as well as from corner to corner. When you sit on the chair, or press on the seat, you should never feel the springs and it should never squeak. If you can see the springs through the upholstery, forget it; this is a poorly made chair. Also beware of nails or staples showing.

It almost seems silly to say this, but always sit in a chair before buying it. Check for firmness or softness to see which suits your comfort best. The important thing is that it feels good. No springs or hard edges, no lumps or bumps.

Pick up one end of the chair. It shouldn't squeak. Check the underside for raveled fabric, excess glue or rough wood. Does it feel solid when you lift it or lean on the back when all four feet are on the floor?

Check out the fabric. What you're looking for is good tailoring, no puckering or loose threads, and patterns that match on seats, side arms and back. Any trimmings should be sewn on securely and straight. Skirts should hang straight with crisp corners and the fabric should be lined.

Club Chair

Large, overstuffed armchairs are often referred to as club chairs. They encourage lounging, and if you place an ottoman in front of one of these comfortable chairs, you can create the perfect spot for doing just that.

Slipper Chair

This chair is smaller in scale than the club chair, usually armless and shorter than most chairs. The back is also

lower than your average chair. The original use for a slipper chair was for drawing up close to the fireplace. It is equally at home in the living room and the bedroom and usually stands alone. You don't often see several used in the main sitting or conversation area, but they are wonderful to draw into the group for extra seating, or for their original purpose. I have two in my living room and find them extremely convenient, as you can perch on the edge or turn easily to face people on either side of you.

Interior decorator Billy Baldwin was famous for his small-scaled slipper chairs with white slipcovers or upholstery. They were his signature and he had them in his New York City apartment as well as in his vacation home on Nantucket Island. They provide a wonderful solution for an arrangement where larger chairs might be too cumbersome. Singing the praises of the slipper chair, Mark Hampton says it is as popular today as it was a hundred years ago. Good design always prevails.

Wing Chair

A wing chair is graceful and almost architectural in design. Place it opposite a fireplace and it becomes the coziest spot to curl up with a book on a winter's evening. "Put it in front of a bay window and suddenly you've got a corner office," says New York interior designer Vicente Wolf. A wing chair is perfect for adding height and drama to a room. It can be upholstered in leather, which is a popular version, or a more refined fabric such as velvet or heavy tapestry in flame stitch patterns.

Use one wing chair by itself. Or use two, placed opposite each other on either side of a fireplace or across from a sofa with a table between. A wing chair is adaptable and can be used in contemporary or traditional settings. Larger ones are used in living rooms, while smaller versions are popular for bedrooms.

There's a chair for every occasion. They come in all different sizes, styles, shapes, fabrics and colors. Choose the one that suits your needs and space. The illustrations opposite show just a few.

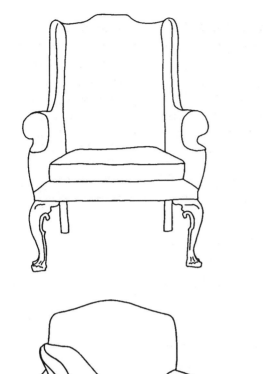

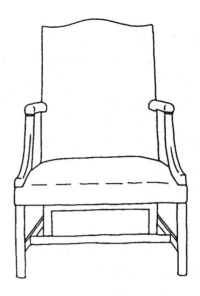

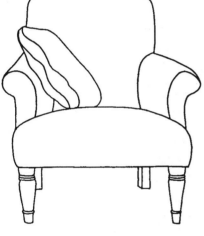

Occasional Chairs

These chairs are usually smaller than upholstered chairs and have a wood frame. There are many styles that can add accents and complement a room. An occasional chair is quite versatile, as it can be placed against a wall and easily brought into the main conversation area when extra seating is needed.

Chair Styles

Whether your style is country or formal, you'll find a myriad of occasional wood frame chairs. These chairs are available not only in furniture showrooms, but at flea markets, auctions and antique shops. If you can't afford a real antique Shaker ladderback, or Windsor or Queen Anne side chair, for example, there are reproductions available in almost any style. It's often hard to differentiate between the original and the copy.

Most American chair styles are based on English furniture. The best woodworkers tried to reproduce the fine craftsmenship of the original chairs. Other furniture makers adapted the styles, simplified the decoration and produced country style chairs and tables. Some very elegant furniture evolved out of the "country furniture" tradition, notably Shaker furniture and Windsor chairs. In the twentieth century, other influences inspired furniture designers. The Art Nouveau and Art Deco art movements produced furniture that is still popular. Innovative designs were created by architects Frank Lloyd Wright, Marcel Breuer and Mies van der Rohe. Designer Charles Eames designed chairs made of molded and shaped plywood and plastic that opened up new ways of creating furniture. Currently, artists are producing highly individual pieces of furniture that have become known as "Studio" furniture.

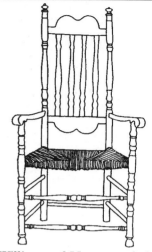

William and Mary armchair

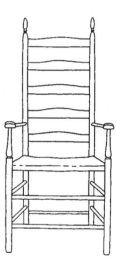

Shaker armchair

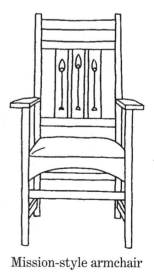

Mission-style armchair

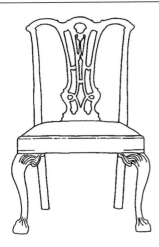

Chippendale side chair

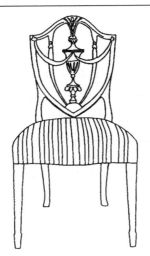

Federal side chair

Windsor side chair

Windsor armchair

Sheraton side chair

Bentwood side chair

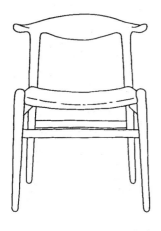

Danish modern side chair

Molded-plywood chair

Tulip armchair

Tables

Coffee tables, end tables, side tables and library tables are some of the options for the living room or family room. Here, too, you'll find different sizes, styles and construction, but the quality of your tables isn't as crucial as it is for upholstered furniture. A table should be sturdy, functional and appealing. Its size should relate to its use.

Coffee Table

The coffee table, as we know it, is a relatively new creation. After 1915, the low table in front of a sofa came into being for holding books, magazines, beverages and flowers, as well as for propping one's feet upon. Before this, decorative painted metal trays were placed on a stand in front of sofas or chairs. The low coffee table was favored by designers as the alternative to its more

Guidelines

1. An end table should measure 2 inches higher or 2 inches lower than the arms of the sofa or chair. Its major purpose is for holding a lamp. The height of the lamp affects the height of the table, and vice versa.
2. A coffee table is usually as high as or slightly lower than the seat cushions of the sofa or chairs.
3. A tea table is approximately 23 inches high.

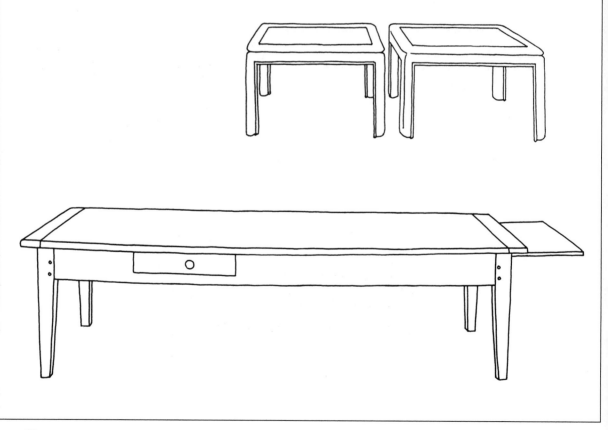

refined cousin, the tea table. The tea table, which is generally higher, is often found in Victorian-style rooms and set in front of a straight-back settee. The low coffee table, with an average height of 15 inches, contributes to a more relaxing atmosphere and is the most obvious piece of furniture around which to arrange a sofa and chairs.

Alternatives to Traditional Coffee Tables: Ottomans, dining tables cut down to size, nesting tables, small tables of the same size placed side by side, a pedestal or large clay planter turned upside down and outfitted with a thick glass top, and a trunk suggest just a few of the ways you can create interesting tables. Wrought-iron garden tables make interesting coffee tables as well. If you find one in a yard sale but the frame is rusted and the top missing, it's easy to restore with spray paint and a piece of wood or glass cut to fit the top.

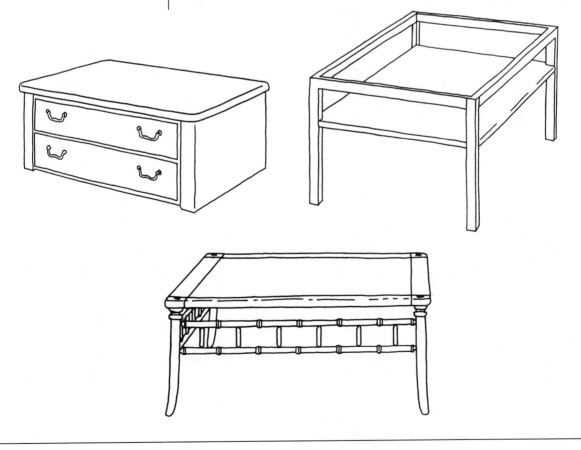

Tea Tables

These tables are higher than coffee tables, 23 or 24 inches, and often smaller as well. They are perfect in front of a settee or straight-back chairs and can double as eating tables in small rooms that serve many purposes. A tea table is perfect in an apartment that lacks a dining room. No matter what style of furnishings you've chosen, even if it's contemporary, an antique tea table is a nice small piece to consider as an interesting focal point or accent in a room. It can be used as is, or covered with a linen tea cloth or a full tablecloth hanging to the floor.

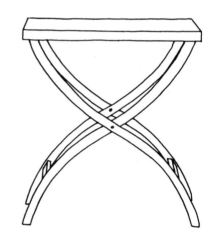

Occasional Tables

End tables, placed at either end of a sofa, are a relatively new invention, part of the twentieth century. They are used primarily for holding lamps, and while they often match, it isn't a necessity for good design. End tables don't even have to be made especially for that purpose.

I found a lovely tea table in a secondhand shop ("antiques shop" would elevate it beyond its station). It has a wooden Victorian-style base that I painted light gray. The top is a separate oval piece of beveled marble. I use it as an end table to hold a lamp and a few interesting objects.

Be creative, using an antique piece or something that wasn't originally intended as a table at all. A sewing cabinet, for example, might make an interesting side table, as would a dry sink, an unusual plant stand or a serving cart from another era. Hand-stenciled and painted work tables from the 1800s are quite popular as end tables for sofas and bedsides. They often have a single drawer with a small, rectangular top. Those made in New England and Pennsylvania between 1820 and 1840 are currently in demand.

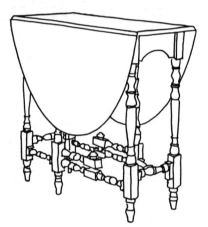

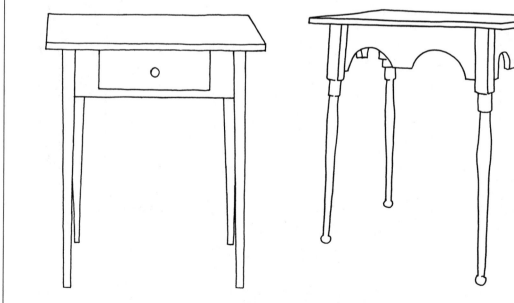

All-Purpose Tables

A library table is usually long and narrow and can be placed against a wall or behind a sofa for holding lamps, books, flowers or collections. These tables are wonderfully practical in the dining room for serving buffets or in a hallway, as well as the living room. Aside from being good-looking, a library table is a handy piece of furniture to press into service for holiday entertaining, even if, at this point, a party is the furthest thing from your mind.

Another table that could work well in a living room might be an occasional drop leaf that takes up little space when the leaves are folded but can be expanded to accommodate various uses. A large round table is often used in a corner or next to a sofa. If it is made of beautiful wood, leave it bare; if not, cover it with a pretty floor-length tablecloth. The top is of ample size to hold a lamp, a vase of flowers, a stack of books and some framed photographs.

Purchasing Furniture Little by Little

If you can't afford to buy everything at once, don't despair. Often the success of a decorating project is due to the fact that it was done slowly. It's a good idea to live with each piece of furniture as it is introduced into the space before adding another. It's also good to know you can do a lot with a few pieces of furniture, such as an upholstered sofa or love seat, two wooden chairs and a tea table or coffee table. Rather than concentrating on the fact that the room is bare, look at one area as if it were the entire room for now. If you have a focal point, such as a fireplace, arrange a conversation area around it with these pieces. You'll be surprised at how livable you can make this one area. Try each piece in different positions. Sit in each chair or on the sofa. Imagine how the arrangement will function with other people. Then you can take your time to look at the rest of the room in the same way before tying it all together. Once you've chosen those first few pieces, everything else that follows should relate to them, so choose these items with care.

If the room still looks bare, fill in with inexpensive pieces that may eventually move to other areas of your home. There are also ways to fill in with color, pattern and inexpensive accessories for effect. These might include throw pillows, a wallhanging, framed posters, books, flowers, plants, lamps and collectibles that don't cost a lot but look good.

Decorators have varying opinions about how you should furnish an entire home. Some think it's best to buy one or two essential items for each room; others think it's best to complete one room before moving to another. Some think you should purchase all the large and more expensive items first, because the less significant things will fall into place as you find them. Since

Decorator Michael Formica says, "Buy larger than you think. If you think a table will be too large in your space, once you get it home you'll be surprised at how well it works."

most people moving into their first home are on a limited budget, the most practical and often the only option is buying little by little. Having an overall plan, however, ensures that you will make fewer mistakes, thus getting the most for your money. In this way, you won't buy a sofa that's the wrong size, shape and color, just because it's on sale.

Creative Arrangements

A couple just moved into a new home with a sofa, a chair and a few odds and ends. "We have everything lined up against the wall," they said. "How should we arrange things?"

A living room needs breathing room. It's a good idea to start by moving the sofa and chair away from the walls. Placing a few pieces on the diagonal, with room to walk around each piece, will help make a sparse room seem fuller. Try placing a desk or long, narrow table against a wall or behind the sofa, and arrange a lamp, a few objects or books and a vase of flowers on it. This will make the room seem more furnished than it might be. Try a cozy, tight arrangement away from the wall, even if your room is rather large. For a small room you might place the sofa against the wall with the other pieces perhaps angled to face the sofa, but not against the opposite wall. A large potted tree with an uplight is a great way to fill an empty corner. An uplight is a canister light about 8 inches high that can sit on the floor or table.

Living Rooms for Multiple Purposes

For those with smallish houses, rooms have to do double duty. Carefully selected furnishings and lots of good storage are the keys to making it work. When planning

Tip
Put something in every room that doesn't seem to belong. It will take away the stiffness of the space. A room shouldn't look too coordinated.

the living room in their new house, an architect and his wife made sure to provide plenty of storage space for their six-year-old daughter and her toys and collections. If you have plenty of storage in your first home, they advise, it will be your last. It's hard to move away from a well-planned house. They bought lots of Rubbermaid plastic boxes that fit into the cabinets under the windows that surround the room. Lots of "stuff" is easily stowed behind closed doors. By day their living room functions as a place for children to play. For an evening of adult entertaining there is never a trace of "kiddy litter."

Sometimes an outdoor porch or deck provides extended living room space in warm climates. The new wicker furniture is a good choice for indoor and outdoor use. In this way you can move the furniture around to suit your needs. If you use your outdoor room for several months of the year, furnish it as an extension of the living room. The fabrics and colors you choose should go with the living room.

In newly built homes, what used to be the living room is often referred to as a great room. These rooms are favored by families with small children because they serve as recreation rooms as much as places to entertain. An armoire, entertainment unit or bookcase functions well here, providing neat storage for everyone's needs. If you don't yet have children but think you might in the near future, consider this when making your purchases. A glass-top coffee table with sharp corners might tempt you now, but you may regret this purchase when you have a toddler.

Lighting

Lighting is trickier than most of us realize. Different types of lighting are needed for different situations, and it's not so simple to know what you need where. Lighting changes the mood of a room. It makes you feel safer. It helps you perform tasks better. Don't think it's a deficiency if you go into a lighting store and haven't a clue. The biggest mistake most people make is choosing the wrong type of lighting for a room. What should you do?

Light It Right

Each room needs lighting for the activities you do there. A kitchen obviously needs different lighting than a living room. A good home lighting plan considers both natural light and artificial light. Here's a list of questions to answer for each room. Keep in mind there may be more than one answer for each question.

1. What do you do there?

2. What kind of ambience do you want to create?

3. Are there areas that require more than one type of lighting?

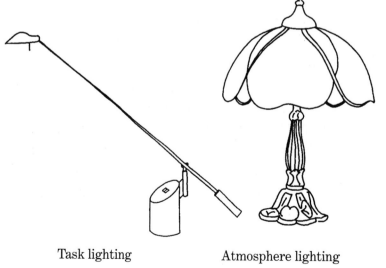

Task lighting   Atmosphere lighting

Tip

The American Lighting Association says there are three types of lighting that work together to light a room: general, task and accent. A good lighting plan combines all three for function and style. Some rooms or areas need all three for different times and activities.

Types of Lighting

General

This type of lighting provides overall comfort. For example, use ceiling fixtures in hallways and over stairs and entrance ways to light these areas evenly. In the dining room, a chandelier will give you general lighting, but if it's on a dimmer switch, it can also be lowered for ambient light. Wall-mounted fixtures or recessed or track lights will give general lighting to a room.

Task Lighting

When you have to balance a checkbook or prepare dinner you want a lot of light on the subject. For these tasks use recessed or track lighting or a portable lamp. "Bright" is the operative word.

Accent Lighting

When you want to highlight and create drama, you want an accent light. This requires at least three times more light than general lighting. If you have a painting on the wall, accent it with track, recessed or wall-mounted fixtures.

Lighting Systems

Portable Lamps

These offer the most versatility in a room. The height and shade are important considerations. A parchment shade will allow the light to center down on the table or up on the ceiling, but won't give you ambience. A translucent shade will give you a strong downlight and uplight as well as diffused ambient light through the shade.

Track Lighting

Popular for task and general lighting, this is a very flexible system. Each light can be positioned on the track in any direction, so you can fiddle with the lighting until you get it the way you want it.

Recessed Lighting

This is a very streamlined way to have all three types of lighting. Recessed fixtures can be used anywhere and are installed in the ceiling with only the rim showing. They're perfect for low ceiling areas and over kitchen counters where you need focused downlights.

Instant Romance

Dimmer switches have to be the best invention since the lightbulb. Also called rheostats, they enable you to lower the amount of light from a lamp. A bright light for reading can be dimmed for romance once you curl up on your new sofa for an evening with a significant other.

The Cool and Hot News

Fluorescent light produces cool light. It's very harsh and makes your skin look green. In other words, never, ever use it in the dining room, bedroom or anywhere else you want to look good. It's usually used in the kitchen or garage because it's bright. Incandescent light is warmer and adds a little glow. Use it for Hollywood-style makeup lights around your bathroom mirror and you'll leave home feeling good about yourself.

Where to Find It
Call 1-800-274-4484 for an American Lighting Association showroom near you. For an extensive color catalog of discount lamps and lighting fixtures, call 800-735-3377, fax 910-882-2262 or e-mail your request to gvlight@aol.com.

Accessories

At this point your room may be furnished but seem unfinished. It may even look as though no one lives there. Rooms come to life when you add expressions of individual character. Accessories are the incidental objects that are generally smaller than furniture and don't fall exactly into the category of utilitarian. They might include artwork, collectibles, clocks, vases and plants. In short, they are the finishing touches.

Accessories and artwork are easy to move about, add to or eliminate if they don't look good. Accessories can be objects with sentimental or personal value and can be added without your worrying about detracting from the overall scheme.

If you already own a painting, for example, you can plan artwork to go in specific areas before placing the furniture or choosing the fabrics. However, it is more common to design and furnish your rooms, then add the art where it looks best.

Favorite Things

It can be a lot of fun arranging and rearranging the things you love. Keep in mind the same principles that you applied to arranging the furniture: balance and scale. One of my favorite decorators likes to create what he calls "tablescapes." That is, he arranges groupings of items as if for a still life painting. The items might relate in color, size, texture or subject matter. Here's how it works: Start with an occasional table on which you might place a beautiful plate with a floral design that reflects the colors in the room. Next to this place a vase of fresh flowers or a flowering plant in a lovely cachepot, a grouping of family photographs in interesting frames and an antique ceramic box. In this arrangement you have different textures, heights, colors and patterns that relate and work well together.

In another scene you might have a collection of Staffordshire dogs, for example. Rather than placing them in different spots around the room, try grouping them together for more impact. Putting a collection all together makes a strong statement. A collection of pretty blue-and-white plates is dramatic when displayed on a wall in a blue-and-white room.

I have a collection of old candlesticks. Some are silver and very ornate, others are made of brass, and some were wooden thread spools from the early part of the century. I like using them as often as possible and display them as a grouping on a sideboard in the living room. Sometimes I use just a few of them on the dining table when I have company.

A decorator friend makes arrangements with neutral colors. He likes wooden objects and uses them with anything made of leather. The arrangement changes from time to time, depending on the objects he's uncovered in his foraging at flea markets and in antique shops. Adding accessories can be an ongoing activity and keeps a room looking fresh.

Flowers, Plants and Small Trees

Plants and trees add color, height and liveliness where needed. For example, you might use a large ficus tree to fill an empty corner or create a garden area with large potted plants on a tea cart. You can never go wrong with a vase filled with fresh flowers. I have a favorite glass vase in which I almost always have in-season flowers. This is an easy way to change colors on that particular table, but flowers always fit in with my living room color scheme.

Tip
Decorative accessories should come as a surprise. They shouldn't scream out for attention but rather should be discovered.

Useful Collectibles

Baskets, bowls and boxes make good-looking accessories that are also practical. There are collections that are simply for display and others that are good-looking and useful. In a country house with rafters, you often see handmade rustic baskets hanging. When a basket is needed, it's easy to reach up and pick the right one for the job. An interesting basket can hold an arrangement of dried flowers or foods such as onions and garlic in the kitchen, or can be used as a serving container.

Antiques

It's easy to add interest and character with antique accessories. These are usually items that are purchased as we stumble on them. One area of affordable antiques is American folk art. Items such as weathervanes and whirligigs, maritime artifacts such as boat models and ship compasses, early quilts and hooked rugs are prized for their charm and whimsy. If you want to introduce antique collectibles to your decor, there are lots of books and information about items that may interest you.

Books

Books add color and texture and make a room feel lived in. Use them in bookcases, piled haphazardly or arranged neatly on a table, or placed about the room. I have a small child-size chair next to the fireplace where I keep whatever current books I'm reading. Books give a room instant character.

Tip
When buying antiques, do your homework. Study antique magazines, go to auction houses and know what you want to spend for an item before attending the auction. If you overpay for something, it won't give you the pleasure for which it was intended.

Storage Units

Storage units should be selected to store specific items. Storage systems usually offer standard components grouped together. A storage unit to store the television, VCR and electronic equipment is a good item to consider. These usually take up a lot of wall space, so you'll need your notebook and measurements when going shopping. If you don't have an unobstructed wall, but only a narrow area, for example, between two win-

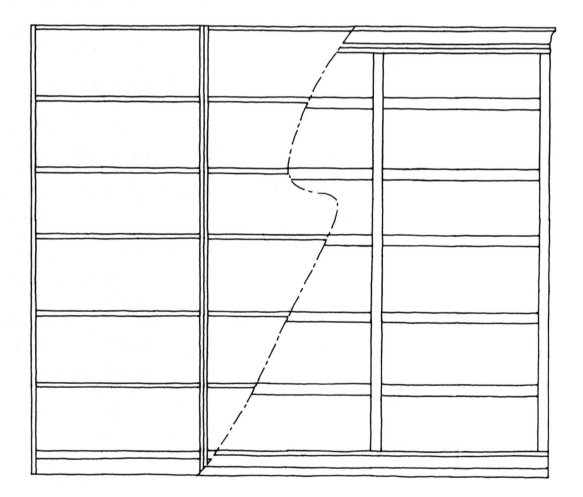

Make a plain bookcase (left) look built-in (right) with molding at top,
facings on shelves and baseboard at bottom.

dows, consider a bookcase to hold these items. There are so many different cabinets made for storage that it's just a matter of deciding where to put what and how much space you want to devote to it. A corner cupboard is another option. With a cabinet underneath open shelves, a corner cupboard utilizes dead corner space efficiently.

Insufficient closet and storage space is the most common complaint about most houses and apartments. Before buying a storage unit, determine what you need to store in the living room or family room, where it will be situated (ideally, for home entertainment, it should be opposite the seating area) and what will look good with the design of the room.

If you like the look of built-ins but your budget can't handle hiring a carpenter to achieve this, you can get the look without the expense. Measure your wall area from side to side and floor to ceiling. Buy the most inexpensive bookshelves you can find, to fill the space as much as possible. Then attach a facing piece, which could be a strip of wood such as a 1 x 4 , and a strip of molding across the top. Add boards as filler down the left and right sides. Attach a baseboard across the bottom, thus facing the entire unit. Add vertical strips of wood where the bookcases join and, if desired, to the front edges of the shelves. This could be a decorative molding. Paint the entire unit the color of the walls and it will look like a custom built-in.

The Kitchen

The kitchen is the hub of a home. It's usually the room in which we spend the most amount of time. It is also the first room most people want to renovate. These rooms are like computers—they need upgrading every time you turn around. But that's a major investment in the realm of renovating and unless you've bought a house with this in the financial plan, maybe all you need, for now, is a fresh coat of paint. If the cabinets are old and dark, they can be stripped and refinished, or removed and replaced with open shelves, or the cabinet doors can be replaced with glass-front doors. Perhaps all you need to spruce up the old cabinets is new, modern door handles or knobs. Renovating a kitchen is a job for a professional kitchen planner. There are individual contractors as well as companies that specialize in kitchen renovations. If putting in a new kitchen is part of your first-home project, you would do well to consult a local outfit that will work with you to create your dream kitchen within your budget.

If, however, you've just moved into a new home, chances are your kitchen was one of the things that attracted you to the place and the reason you chose it. Think about what you like best about your kitchen and how you want to use this room, and decorate accordingly. People who enjoy cooking have definite ideas about how a good kitchen should function. This is the room that gets filled with good smells and warm feelings, so whether it's a tiny galley kitchen or a family-size room with an eat-in area, you'll want to arrange your things for optimum pleasure and efficiency.

Tip
Make a home sparkle by cleaning the windows. It really makes a big difference.

Tip
If you plan to use yellow for the kitchen walls, select the shade you like and either test it on the wall or go one or two shades lighter. Yellow tends to look much brighter on the wall than on a paint chip.

Use a reputable brand-name paint. This isn't where you want to save pennies. Once the job is done, you want it to last.

Paint Color

Unless your home is brand new, chances are the kitchen will need a coat of paint. Glossy or semigloss paint is a good choice because it can be wiped clean easily. What colors work best in the kitchen? Since this is a much-used room, you want it to be bright and cheerful. When choosing a color, look at it in the daylight and in artificial light, as it will look different. Next, take the size of the room into consideration.

White will make everything look brighter. Lemon yellow makes a room sunny and bright, which is the reason it's so popular for kitchen walls. Pale celery green is lovely and new with wood trim and cabinets painted white. If the walls are painted white, consider using an accent color on the wood trim. Bright white on the ceilings will reflect light.

If you opt for color on the walls, bring home paint chips from the store and, if possible, have a small amount mixed. Try it on one strip of a wall and live with it before making the final commitment.

Faux Finishes

Ragging, sponging, combing and dragging are painting techniques suitable for decorating your walls. A stencil design can be used around walls, doors and window trim and is an easy project as well as a good substitute for wallpaper. (See directions beginning on page 219.)

Wallpaper

Transform a dull kitchen with wallpaper. This is an easy do-it-yourself project, but be sure to choose a prepasted paper and be sure it's washable. There are many vinyl-coated papers to choose from, and these are easy to clean with a damp sponge when the walls get greasy.

Wallpaper borders come in different widths and a variety of designs. They are easy to put up wherever you want a decorative touch. This might be around the window or door, on the narrow wall space above the countertop, around the top of the walls or as a chair rail in the eating area. Consider wallpapering the bottom portion of the wall under the border to delineate an eating area. See page 223 for how to hang wallpaper.

Reclaiming Old Cabinets

Stripping, sanding and painting cabinets is a relatively simple job and an easy way to have a new looking kitchen. If two people do it together, it shouldn't take more than a weekend. This is a good way to save money, es-

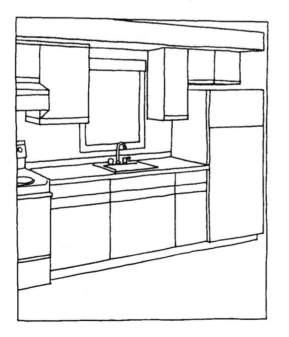

online help
Kitchen Net
www.kitchen-bath.com
This is sponsored by Home Depot. If you are thinking about doing anything yourself to fix up your house, check in here first. There are lots of tips on do-it-yourself projects and design and decorating. Check it out, then climb into your pickup truck, go to Home Depot and drive away with an entire kitchen or bath.

Stock Cabinets: These come in standard sizes. They are less expensive than custom-built cabinets.

Semi-custom Cabinets: These come in standard sizes, but can be slightly customized within a limited range of options.

Custom Cabinets: These are built to order, and you will have a wide range of sizes and finishes available to fit your space and usage. Plan to wait two to three months for these.

pecially if the old kitchen could do with new appliances. Rather than spend money on new cabinets, spend it on appliances. Once the old finish is stripped away, you can restain in a wood color of your choice or faux finish, or paint them to look new. If you want to lighten dark cabinets quickly and easily once they've been sanded down to the raw wood, give them a whitewash. Mix equal parts of white alkyd enamel and paint thinner. Brush the mix into the wood, let it set for five to ten minutes and, using dry cheesecloth, wipe off the excess. Let this dry overnight. Apply a coat of nonyellowing semi-gloss polyurethane to protect the finish.

Replacing Cabinets

You can create a kitchen with a custom look by replacing your old cabinets with up-to-date, modern stock cabinets at surprisingly affordable prices. Unlike custom cabinets, which are built to fit specific spaces, stock cabinets come in standard widths, with filler strips provided to fill in the gaps. You can customize the cabinets with molding prefinished to match the cabinet finishes. You'll find matching material to give your refrigerator a built-in look and a trim kit to give your dishwasher a custom look. Stock cabinets and accessories are sold at home centers, and it's a good idea to look closely at floor samples and know your needs.

Hardware

Details like hardware give a kitchen character. For relatively little cost you can change the knobs on cabinet doors, drawer pulls and sink fixtures. You'll find a wide variety at most home centers or through mail order catalogs. Reproductions of old fixtures can make a new kitchen more interesting. They are available from Renovator's Supply House and other companies.

Floors

Your kitchen floor covering is important. This is where you want good looks, practicality and comfort. You may do a lot of standing while preparing meals in this room. You want the floor to be resilient and easy to clean. This is where you might be feeding pets and children. Is this also a play area? Is this where you'll be eating as well as cooking?

If you don't like what's on the floor, you can redo it. Here are your options: brick, slate, hardwood, linoleum, tile, carpet, vinyl, stone, terrazzo. Most floor-covering projects should be done by a professional. However, if your budget can't handle this but your floor is really terrible, I would suggest putting down vinyl sheet flooring (which requires a professional) or vinyl tiles that are individually glued to subflooring, which can be installed by the do-it-yourselfer. If you think this is the old linoleum your parents or grandparents had in their home, you'll be happy to know it isn't. Vinyl flooring has come a long way. Aside from colors and designs, you can choose a pattern that simulates the look of wood, marble, tile or brick; sometimes it's hard to distinguish it from the real thing.

A Splash of Color

Ceramic tiles come in a variety of colors, patterns and sizes, and there are tile shops all over the country. If you want to spruce up a dull kitchen, consider adding interest to backsplashes with tiles. You might also create a scene with tiles, such as a basket of flowers, or a grouping of fruit, on the wall in back of the range, for example. A visit to a tile center will stimulate your imagination, and you can learn a lot from the sales people, who are generally quite knowledgeable.

Interior designer Barbara Barry says, "Different values of the same colors such as we find in nature are interesting."

Counters

There are many material choices for countertops, and if you're planning to redo yours, you will want to look into the advantages and disadvantages of those you are most attracted to. Favorites are Formica, Corian, butcher block, stainless steel and tile. You want your countertops to be practical for their specific uses.

Storage Space

The success of any kitchen is measured in adequate storage and this translates into proper storage for each work area of the kitchen. If there is an island, for example, you'll want a drawer for utensils. Pots and pans should be close to the stove. An eating counter needs a drawer for linens and flatware. Food that doesn't go in the refrigerator must be stored conveniently if you don't have a pantry for this purpose. The sink needs a cabinet for cleaning supplies and a garbage pail.

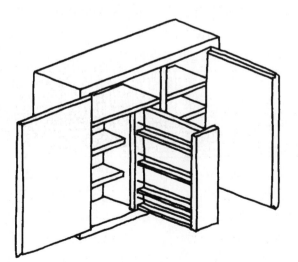

The Small Kitchen

With good planning, a small kitchen can function efficiently. Every square inch must count, but this doesn't mean it can't be smart and sophisticated. In this case I think it's best to think sleek rather than country cluttered for your decor.

Open shelves make a small kitchen look airy, but this also means you have to be extra neat and tidy because everything is on display. Paint everything glossy white and keep the walls unfussy. Countertops should be clear of accessories and small appliances if possible. Cooking utensils can be hung on a wall rack or placed in a crock on the counter to free up cabinet and drawer space. Display your most interesting kitchen utensils in pitchers and crocks, leaving room in drawers. Use baskets, colanders and bowls to hold fruit and vegetables that don't need refrigeration. An inexpensive wire rack placed over a stack of dinner plates on a shelf can provide a smaller shelf for bowls. Look for convenient inserts such as dividers, pullout trays and lazy Susans at home centers.

If appliances need replacing, look for small-size units. Almost every major appliance company makes small versions of their larger models.

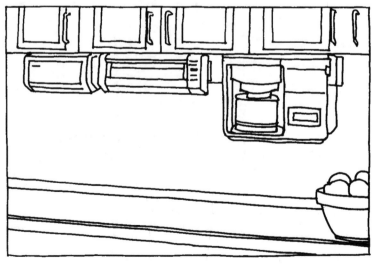

Expanding Counter Space

In a room without a lot of counter space, the rolling cabinet or island creates temporary work areas wherever needed. If it's possible to mount a drop-leaf table on one end of a counter, it can give you extra temporary space when needed. A small table strategically placed will add counter space and, if possible, storage space. Look for a small end table with a drawer and cabinet or open shelf below. It will look good and serve a practical purpose.

Efficiency Ideas

If you're looking to make an existing kitchen more efficient, here are a few ideas that that won't require you to spend a lot of money.

● Hang a pot rack overhead to free up cabinets and drawers.

● Use dead space with a corner shelf unit .

● Put up a narrow shelf to hold cookbooks within reach.

● Undercabinet lighting is easy to install. Look for these task lights in home centers.

● Hang a small, narrow shelf for holding spices and herbs on the wall above the backsplash.

● Instead of curtains, mount a glass shelf across the window at the sash for holding pots of fresh herbs at your fingertips. It's a great look, especially in an all-white kitchen where you might want to add touches of green.

● Fit cabinets with tall, narrow compartments to hold such items as trays, cutting boards and cookie tins.

● Use clear glass apothecary and Mason jars to hold rice, pasta and beans on an open shelf.

- Mount a spice holder on the inside of a cabinet door.

- Hang a Shaker peg rack on a narrow wall or the back of a door for holding aprons, pot holders or baskets of potatoes and onions.

- Use a large wooden salad bowl or ceramic tureen to hold cleanup items such as a sponge, soap and a scrub brush.

- Mount plastic-coated wire shelves on a wall for holding canisters, and suspend pots, pans and lids below with S hooks.

Appliances

Replacing appliances in your first home might be the very thing that brings a dated-looking kitchen into the twenty-first century. Before buying an appliance, do your homework. Research the different types, styles, sizes and functions, and choose the one that best suits your needs within your budget. Some appliances are more important than others in the scheme of things, but you have to decide where to put your money.

For example, when a couple moved into their new house, they needed a washer and dryer and a new dishwasher. They didn't think the washer and dryer had to have all sorts of cycles and, in fact, opted for a combined stack unit because they needed to conserve space. However, they did want a whisper-soft dishwasher and one that was state of the art. If space saving is a consideration, look for small appliances that can substitute for major appliances. For example, a bar-type under-the-counter refrigerator might be all you need for now, and it will cost much less than a full-size refrigerator.

Microwave and toaster ovens are other options for cooking. On the other hand, if cooking is your thing,

Appliance help
Many appliance manufacturers have more than one brand, so the 800 numbers for different brands may be the same. If you are looking for product literature, advice on installation or operation, repairs or service, or dealer locations, call anytime.

Admiral 800-688-9900
Amana 800-843-0304
Caloric 800-843-0304
Frigidaire 800-451-7007
GE 800-626-2000
Gibson 800-458-1445
Hotpoint 800-626-2000
Jenn-Aire 800-688-1100
Kelvinator 800-323-7773
KitchenAid 800-422-1230
Magic Chef 800-688-1120
Maytag 800-688-9900
Modern Maid 800-843-0304
RCA 800-626-2000
Roper 800-447-6737
Speed Queen 800-843-0304
Sub-Zero 800-444-7820
Tappan 800-537-5530
Whirlpool 800-253-1301
White-Westinghouse 800-245-0600

Money-Saving Tip
Old appliances that still work
can be transformed with spray
paint made especially for this
purpose in a wide variety of
colors. An old white porcelain
sink can be resurfaced.

**When buying an oven
range, the depth and width
of the hood should match
that of the range.**

For information on buying
appliances: There's a book
called *Consumer Guide to
Home Energy Savings,* pub-
lished by the American Council
for an Energy Efficient Econ-
omy. It lists the most efficient
units for eight kinds of
appliances grouped by size and
fuel type and is available in
most bookstores.

you might want to look into replacing your existing
stove with a commercial range. Until recently, commercial gas ranges were designed for restaurants, but more
and more homeowners are installing them. Some models are oversized, so make sure you have enough room
in back and on each side to accommodate the unit. Range
widths run from 30 to 62 inches. Some manufacturers
have come out with a commercial range for the home
that fits into a standard 24-inch depth. Keep in mind
that it's heavier than a normal range and needs suffi-
cient support and an adequate exhaust system.

Eat-in Space

Some kitchens are the kinds of rooms you never want
to leave. A kitchen with an eat-in area is ideal. It usually means there is plenty of space in which to work,
entertain and eat, with places for everything. In this
case you'll want to decorate it in a way that reflects
your style. No matter how you've planned to decorate
the rest of the house, this room can be an extension of
that style or can be treated in a completely different
way. For example, a couple are decorating their first
home with traditional furnishings but always dreamed
of a cozy country kitchen. While the rest of the house is
light and airy with chintz fabrics and highly polished
floors, the kitchen is painted barn red. They have a pine
farm table in the eat-in area with wonderful old mismatched chairs they found in antiques shops and at yard
sales. They had fun stripping and repainting them in
their spare time. The seats all have calico cushions, and
homespun fabric was used to make café curtains. "This
is where I like to display my country collections," she
says, "and everyone is always surprised when they come
into this room."

While you want to make your work area in the kitchen as efficient as possible, your eating area can be less "kitcheny" and more homey. There are many special kitchen and bath books and magazines for you to look through in order to get ideas. Remember, used kitchen chairs of every conceivable style are the easiest pieces of furniture to find. Table and chairs don't have to match. In fact, sometimes it's more interesting when they don't. However, you can find a variety of affordable tables in different sizes—round, rectangular, square, oval—to fit within your space and to suit your needs. If, for example, you need more countertop space, consider a table that can be used this way. A marble-top table provides an excellent surface for pastry and bread making. A chopping block surface is perfect for cutting. There are excellent buys in ready-to-finish furniture that can be easily stained, painted or faux finished. This is a good way to save money.

If your eat-in area is too small for a full-size table with room for chairs around it, consider building in a window seat in one corner for seating on two sides of the table.

Many things end up on kitchen counters that would be better put somewhere else. Plan counter space so it is usable, not cluttered.

coffeemaker
toaster
microwave oven
coffee mill
juicer
food processor
blender
container for large spoons, etc.
espresso machine
plants
cookbooks
bread box
fruit bowl
telephone

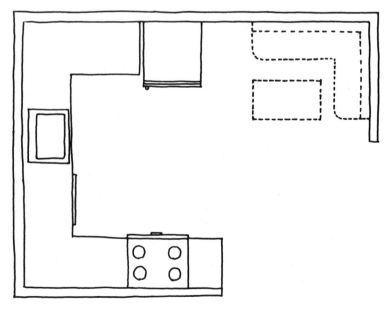

Tip

If you must cover a kitchen window, use materials with low maintenance requirements such as blinds or shades.

Window Treatment

There are as many options for treating your kitchen windows as there are for windows in the rest of your home: curtains, shutters, blinds, shades, swags, valances or nothing at all. If you have a lovely view, don't cover it up. You want as much light to come into your kitchen as possible. Natural lighting is the best lighting of all. However, if you want to soften this area or you need to cover the windows for privacy, minimal treatment is usually best. Whatever your choice, it should be easy to clean.

Café curtains are popular for kitchen windows. For a quick, no-sew café curtain, use two plaid linen dish towels and clip-on curtain rings available wherever sewing supplies are sold. Evenly space the clip-on rings across the top edge of each dish towel. Feed the rings onto a tension curtain rod and place the rod between the window frame at the desired height. Linen dish towels are good-looking and inexpensive. Even if you change the window treatment at some later date, this can work temporarily when you first move in.

Accessories

Placemats, tablecloths, napkins and table accessories add style and hominess to your eat-in area. If you have a white kitchen with stained wood cabinets and wooden furniture, for example, use these items to add color and texture. Other items to consider for a change of look, even from morning to evening, are candles and candleholders, and centerpieces such as a country basket holding pots of geraniums at breakfast and a large country pitcher or vase filled with fresh flowers at dinnertime. Your style of table setting will set the mood for your type of dining.

Lighting

Lighting is most important in the kitchen. You need different types of lighting for different areas, depending on their uses. Recessed lighting spreads illumination evenly and highlights work stations perfectly. But if you don't have such lighting in your kitchen, and since we're not talking here about renovation, you'll want to add what you can to improve the situation. The most efficient method is to add strips of lighting under the wall cabinets or shelves over the counters. These are available in different lengths at home centers. If the overall lighting is poor, you may need to consult an electrician about what kinds of lighting can be installed. This is not a project for the do-it-yourselfer.

A small table lamp on the counter or on a small table in the eating area makes the room cozy and intimate when overhead lights are too harsh. Home centers sell rheostat switches to dim lights so you can control the amount of lighting in the room.

Bring as much natural light into the room as possible by using light colors and not covering windows. If there's a door that obstructs light, consider replacing the wood panels with glass.

Tip
Lamps create more intimate lighting than overhead fixtures.

Getting Organized

When you first move into your first home you'll want to get your kitchen set up as soon as possible. Begin by setting out everything in stacks according to category. Use the floor if you don't have enough counter and table-top space. For example, set out your dinnerware in one area, your glasses in another, your pots and pans in another and so on. Then decide which items should be within easy reach and where they seem most logical. For example, glasses might go on a shelf next to the refrigerator. Pots and pans would be situated next to the stove.

The best access to cabinets is at eye level. Your least-used items should go on the very top and very bottom shelves, as well as at the back of deep shelves. Heavy items are best stored on bottom shelves or in bottom drawers.

Basic Kitchenware

Buy the best cookware you can afford and save money on the less important items such as mixing bowls, measuring spoons, and salad spinner. A vegetable peeler might not seem important, but this is something you'll need, and a good-quality item doesn't cost that much. You'll be glad you spent the five dollars even though you could have gotten one for a dollar fifty. If you're new at this, you might find a checklist of basic items worth taking with you to a good kitchenware shop.

- Two or three different-sized saucepans with lids
- Large pasta pot for boiling water, with a lid
- Set of mixing bowls in graduated sizes
- Roasting pan with a rack
- Coffeepot or electric coffee maker
- Colander
- Slotted spoon
- Spatula
- Serving spoon and fork
- Wire whisk
- Set of wooden spoons
- 1- or 2-cup measuring cup
- Measuring spoons

- Set of knives for paring and carving
- Steak knives
- Cutting board
- Vegetable peeler
- Can opener
- Corkscrew
- Large, medium and small frying pans
- Salad spinner
- If you bake: cookie sheets, pie pans; round, loaf and square baking pans
- Serving tray
- Serving platters
- A twenty-piece standard dinnerware set (five-piece settings for four people)
- Flatware set (usually includes fork, knife, spoon)
- Coffee mugs
- Everyday glasses: juice, water, old-fashioned
- Wine and champagne glasses
- Placemats, tablecloth and napkins
- Candlesticks
- Salt and pepper shakers

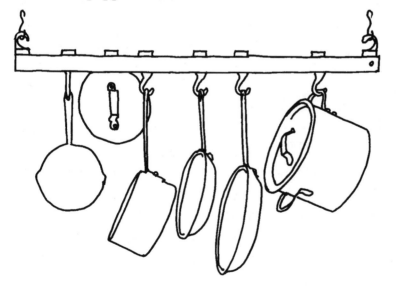

The Dining Room

I think the most civilized design creation is the dining room. Years ago, every respectable house had one. Dining rooms are used for all sorts of family activities that have nothing to do with eating. Kids do homework at the dining room table, families have ongoing games on the dining room table, jigsaw puzzles are left in progress for days on the dining room table, and people spend leisurely Sunday morning breakfasts with the newspaper spread out upon the dining room table.

Unfortunately, when builders save space, the first room they eliminate is the dining room. Eating is relegated to a dining area, which is either an extension of the living room or a space created as part of the kitchen. However, if you're fortunate enough to have this marvelous luxury, you'll want to furnish it in a style that allows it to serve many functions.

When my daughter and her husband moved into their house they practically ignored the dining room. Since they have an eat-in kitchen, the dining room seemed the least important room to fill with furniture they might never use. But then one Christmas they gave a dinner party, and suddenly the dining room demanded attention.

While you might think the dining room is unimportant, once you start using it you'll discover the joy of having any meal, be it breakfast or Thanksgiving dinner, in this room. This is where most of us use things we might have inherited from family members: a lovely lace or crocheted tablecloth, ornate silverware, cut glass goblets, napkin rings and candlesticks, even salt cellars. None of these things seems out of place in the dining room. Of all the rooms in the house, the dining room is perhaps the least likely to be redecorated. It is in this room that you can express your talents with creative table settings, artistically arranged flowers and culinary delights.

The environment in a dining room can be one of relaxed, homey informality or one of a more formal nature. When planning the dining room, think about your lifestyle. Will the room be used for everyday activities as well as meals? How will you entertain? Will you have large family holiday meals here? Do you want your dining room to accommodate large sit-down dinners as well as small intimate ones? Your decorating choices will also be dictated by the other rooms in your home, to some degree. While the dining room can be quite different in style, if it's seen from the living room, for example, you don't want a change that is jarring from one room to the next. They should relate in some way, perhaps by color, furniture style or fabric. The object is to create a dining room that is functional and pleasing. If you have an eat-in kitchen for casual family dining or even informal entertaining, you might want the dining room to be more formally decorated.

Basic Plan

1. Measure the room's dimensions and make a drawing, with windows and doors in position.

2. Before even deciding on what type of furniture you want, you need to know what size it should be. Keep in mind that a table needs enough space all around to push chairs back and for serving access. The recommended distance is about 32 inches from table to wall. Draw your basic table and chairs on your room plan in your notebook. Each place setting needs approximately 20 inches.

3. Decide if the room will be used for other activities besides having meals. This might determine the type of furniture you want. A pine farm table might be more practical than an expensive antique, for example, if it will also be used as a home office desk.

4. Do you already have furniture that will be used in this room, such as a table, occasional chair, a sideboard, corner cupboard or dry sink? Plan where it will be placed and how much room it will take up.

5. Aside from a table and chairs, if you'd like to have a place to put food out for a buffet or to store tableware and linens, this piece of furniture needn't be conventional, especially if you don't have a lot of room. A small dresser with drawers, for example, can hold linens, and an antique or painted occasional piece of furniture might work as a breakfront. A French baker's rack, a tea cart or a bookcase can provide good-looking storage.

Tables and Chairs

Whether your dining space is part of another room or not, you'll need a table of the right size and proportion for the space, as well as chairs to go around it. The shape of a table can be rectangular, square, oval or round. The size can often determine the feeling of the dining style. For example, a round table is the most intimate. Round and square tables suggest informal dining because there is no defined head of the table. Most formal dining is associated with oval or rectangular tables. If you want to accommodate large parties only now and then, consider a table with extension leaves. Where space permits, your dining room furniture might include a buffet or sideboard and a cabinet or china cupboard for storing serving dishes, glasses and linens.

Chairs are among the easiest items to find at yard sales, auctions and flea markets, and they don't have to match. They are also the easiest items to refinish or paint. One summer I furnished a beach house solely with yard sale and auction finds. I found six unmatched wooden chairs of the same average size and painted them all the same color. Then I ragged each one to give it an interesting texture and to tie them together.

Ready-to-finish furniture is not what it used to be. There is more variety and it's better made, and you can find reproductions of antique furniture that, when finished, are hard to tell from the real thing. This is a good way to save money on your overall house-furnishing budget. Looking for bargain substitutes on such items as sofas and other upholstered furniture isn't a good idea, but with dining room tables, chairs, buffets, armoires and other dining room pieces, it is. In fact, buying bargains can make the room more interesting than purchasing a complete matching set.

Decorator Jeffrey Bilhuber says, never use wooden chairs at a wooden table. Painted or upholstered chairs look best with a polished wooden table.

Temporary Furnishing

If you can't furnish the dining room right away, I often recommend using a round patio table or utility table until you have the means to trade up. Conceal it with a floor-length tablecloth, a lovely old quilt or a pretty sheet and nobody will know what's underneath. Pad the table first with a thin layer of quilt batting to give it body (that's the stuffing that goes inside quilts, and it's readily available in different-size packages at all sewing stores).

Ready-made slipcovers for metal folding chairs or cushions on outdoor furniture are good interim solutions. This way you can get away with not furnishing the dining room properly until you're ready. It may look a little sparse, but it won't be empty. And when you decide to furnish the room, put the money into the chairs. You can always cover up a not-so-nice table.

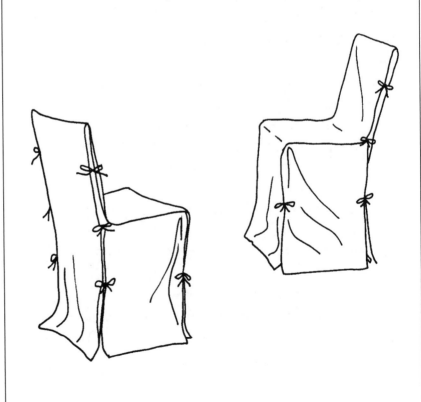

Storage Units

A breakfront, china cabinet, buffet or side table of some sort is an essential piece of furniture for the dining room. If you can find an interesting cabinet with shelves above to hold dishes, doors or drawers below, and a surface for serving or displaying a tea set or other serving pieces, this is ideal. You'll have a practical unit with a focal point of interest for displaying pretty chinaware. Even the top can be used to hold baskets or pieces of pottery or items such as a soup tureen or punch bowl that are used only occasionally. The drawers are handy for holding placemats, napkins and tablecloths or your good silverware.

A storage unit with solid doors below is excellent for storing items used for entertaining such as extra candlesticks, candles, large platters and bowls, serving pieces and vases. A breakfront with glass doors makes a lovely display area for china and glassware. You'll find it extremely convenient to have everything used for entertaining in one place.

Color

Color comes from many sources: paint, wallpaper, fabric, floor covering, table accessories, art. Decide what color scheme suits you and goes with the rest of the rooms. If you're unsure about what to do in the dining room, paint it creamy buttermilk white and you won't go wrong. Paint the wood trim glossy white. Then add color in the fabrics or stick to the soft, monochromatic theme, which will be just as lovely for a brunch as a formal dinner party.

Walls

For quite a while, red was a popular paint color for dining rooms. Now we see very pale sherbet colors coming into vogue. Shades of coral are flattering to food and people. Some decorators are enamored with darkly painted walls, believing them to be the perfect background for the things that make a dining room enchantingly romantic: linens, candlelight, flowers, glass and silverware. Then again, if breakfast and lunches are taken in the dining room, you might want to decorate it to feel as fresh and airy as a summer porch. Dark charcoal might be sophisticated for dinners, but a bit dreary for breakfast. Study the way the light comes into the room at different times of the day before deciding what colors to use.

Wallpaper is is another option for introducing color and texture. Stripes, overall florals, faux finishes and textures such as grass paper are some of your options. Remember, you don't want to ignore the other rooms and you don't want to create a confusing environment. If you choose a patterned wallpaper for this room, you might want solid fabric on your chair cushions or draperies. Or, if the walls are painted, you might want to

Decorator Michael Formica says, "Color is less important than the way light is reflected."

108

use a patterned fabric that picks up some of the same color.

Many dining rooms have wainscoting or a chair rail, which is a molding trim that is applied to the walls partway between the floor and ceiling, about where the top of the chair reaches. It adds a decorative element to walls where there is no particular architectural interest. Sometimes a wallpaper border is used to delineate this area, and a corresponding wallpaper can be applied below or above it with a contrasting paint on the rest of the wall.

Floors

To bare or not to bare? If the floor is made of a good material such as wood or tile and it's in good condition, don't cover it up with wall-to-wall carpeting. Consider an area carpet to soften the room and deaden the sound. If the floor isn't in good condition you might paint it, have wall-to-wall carpeting installed or put down ceramic tiles, vinyl, brick or other natural materials. Whatever your choice of floor cover, it should be practical. While this room doesn't get heavy traffic, there

109

will surely be occasional spills, so white plush carpeting would be impractical. I like a rich Oriental rug in the dining room. It's hard for the average person to tell the difference between the real thing and a good reproduction, which is infinitely more affordable. A textured rug or one with a busy pattern can work well in this room. Another option is a solid color rug with a pattern border that delineates the eating area. Aubusson, Savonnerie or needlepoint rugs would contribute to the look of formal elegance, but they're costly. Sisal is a practical material and quite popular for living and dining rooms if you like a natural look. Dhurries and kilim rugs are produced in India. The designs are usually busy, colorful geometrics. Braided, hooked and rag rugs are options for creating a cozy, casual look.

If your floors are made of wood and they're in good condition, cleaning and waxing might be all that's needed. If the wood is good-looking, either hardwood or pine, for example, but not in top-notch condition, have it professionally sanded (or rent a sander and do it yourself), then refinish it. You can either paint or stain the wood or, as I did recently, simply apply two or three coats of clear polyurethane over the bare wood. This will protect it and the wood will age naturally to a warm color. If you want a light floor, the wood can be bleached or pickled.

Windows

Always consider the window, the style of the room, and the view when choosing a window treatment. Most decorators agree, no treatment is the best treatment of all. If you don't need to cover your windows for privacy, but want to soften this area of the room, swags or valances might be perfect. Other options range from simple blinds, shutters or shades to full drapery treatments.

Carpet types

Saxony: Noted for its elegance and solid colors. Soft and dense, wears well.

Berber: Tweedy, natural colors, large-loop construction. Popular in contemporary homes. Wears well.

Textured: Two-toned tight twist, casual, resists soil. Good for heavily trafficked areas.

Cut Loop: Textured and variegated colors. Sculptured effect. Wears well.

Plush: Luxurious look and feel. Shows footprints easily. Good for bedrooms.

What's the difference between curtains and draperies? Curtains are usually less formal than draperies. Curtains hang from poles or simple curtain rods. Draperies are usually made of heavier fabric and hang from poles and brackets or tracks, and are pulled back, or opened and closed by a rod or pull-cord system. Keep in mind that ready-made draperies are much less expensive than custom-made treatments. Therefore, if you have standard-size windows, you might want to consider a plain treatment such as sheer white panels, which are sure to look good. You can always go back and customize later. Without getting too carried away with every type of fabric treatment available, consider the following options for the dining room.

Fabric

A fabric treatment is the most popular way to surround a window with color, soften a room and turn an ugly duckling into a swan. The right treatment can make windows taller, smaller, wider, less obtrusive or grander than they are. Window treatments can be made from many different fabrics. The fabric you choose for your window treatments can set the mood for the room. If you have windows of different sizes or styles in the room, treating them all the same way will bring everything into harmony.

Floor-to-ceiling draperies

Good for tall windows or a large expanse of window area. These draperies should be lined as sunlight will fade colors in a fabric fairly quickly.

Swags and jabots

The fabric drapes across the top of the window frame and down each side in soft folds. This is a nice way to frame a window with a pretty view and a good use of a printed fabric where you want a touch of color or pattern. The fabric might match the wallpaper or seat cushions, creating an accent around the windows.

Café curtains

A valance and half curtains to the sill are often found in country dining rooms. This type of treatment evokes a casual, informal feeling.

Tiebacks

Curtains made to cover the entire expanse of window when closed can be pulled back gracefully with a tieback and hooked to the window frame. A tieback can be made from the same fabric as the curtain or a contrasting fabric. It can also be a silk cord or wide ribbon. If you use sheer panels, for example, you can tie them back with fabric used elsewhere in the room or with a solid-color fabric to match the walls.

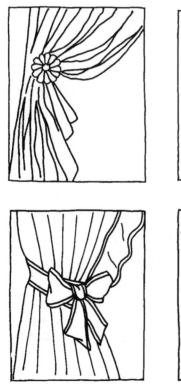
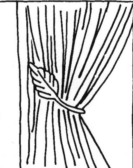

Floor-to-ceiling draperies

Swag and jabots

Tieback panels

Tiered café curtains

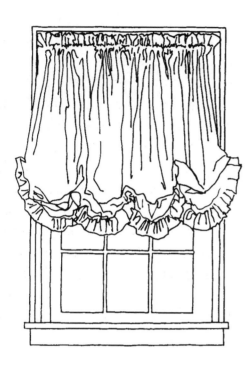

Balloon curtain

Sill-length panels

Scalloped valance

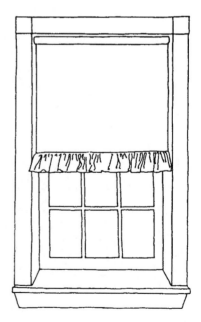

Fabric shade

Fabric Shades

A more tailored approach might be a no-frills fabric shade. One style that I particularly like is the Roman shade, especially made of natural linen. A balloon shade is another option that is quite popular. It is made with cording running through vertical lengths of ring tape that raises and lowers the shade, which usually just covers the window area. The Roman shade rises in tailored, flat pleats, while the balloon shade is more billowy and rises in scalloped poufs. These types of shades are offered in standard sizes and limited but tasteful fabrics through mail-order catalogs. This is an excellent way to have a custom look without the expense. Of course, any of the above can be made to order from your selected fabric through fabric shops and showrooms with decorating/workroom services.

Shutters

We often see shuttered windows on older homes. This is because the casement around the window is deep enough to accommodate the space needed to hold the shutters when opened. Shutters can be solid or louvered. You have the option of covering the lower portion of the window for privacy and adding a valance over the top portion of the window for softening. Or, you can have two sets of shutters or full shutters that fit over the entire window, depending on its size. For nonstandard windows, the shutters would have to be custom-made and costly. Standard-size shutters are available through mail-order catalogs and home centers.

Blinds

Blinds are made of wood, metal, vinyl or stiff fabric. When miniblinds were first introduced, they were extremely popular. They are still a good solution when you want privacy, light control and minimal coverage.

Wooden blinds are currently in vogue. These are not like the old Venetian blinds your grandmother had in her house. These are sleek and sophisticated and come in decorator colors (although white, beige and natural wood tones are still the best-looking), as well as different widths from mini to 2 inches. You also have your choice of different colors for the tape that runs down the front of each side if you want contrast. Go with the same color as your walls for blinds and tape.

Vertical blinds look like they belong in an office. However, like horizontal blinds, these come in a full range of finishes and textures. They offer the ultimate in light and privacy control.

Shades

Pleated fabric shades offer another option for the dining room. Introduced to this country from the Netherlands in the 1970s, they are quite popular for a crisp, carefree, stylish look. A 6-foot fabric shade stacks to under 3 inches, making it a practical treatment where you want to allow for maximum light. The permanent pleats come in 1- and $1^5/_8$-inch widths.

This type of shade is a can't-go-wrong solution to covering windows with a streamlined, good-looking treatment. In fact, when you first move in, measure every window in the house, take these measurements to a home center and order them for all the rooms. In this way your home will have a unified look on the outside and even if you decide to add valances, curtains, drapes or other treatments, this will not be money wasted. It's a good beginning or an end. At a later date you have the option of adding a valance or drapery treatment. If you're moving into a house, not an apartment, the outside of your house will look better if every window is treated the same.

Lighting

A chandelier over the dining table is pretty, but don't rely on it alone to provide lighting. If possible, the chandelier should be on a dimmer so you can adjust the lighting. Flexible lighting is important in the dining room. Some dining rooms have wall lamps or some type of recessed or cove lighting. If you don't have any supplemental lighting, use small table lamps on a sideboard or install wall fixtures. A large mirror, perhaps with an ornate frame over the buffet, is a nice way to decorate a dining room wall. Place lamps on either side.

Every dining room table deserves the romance of candlelight. You can't overdo a good thing. Use lots of candles. This is the best kind of illumination, and you can add as many as there is room for on your table or sideboard. Use candle holders of varying heights; they don't have to match. Have plenty of votive candle holders on hand to add soft low lighting at each place setting.

Setting a Beautiful Table

Nothing is more elegant than a dinner table set with all-white linens and chinaware. A white linen tablecloth sets the background against which you might place a crocheted or lace cover in an eggshell shade. This doesn't have to be an heirloom from your grandmother. There are lots of inexpensive machine-made versions, and you can't tell them from the real thing. This will provide texture with the white background showing through. Creamware plates are lovely with damask napkins. In fact, white patterns of chinaware are classic and some never go out of style. Of all the tableware, whites are usually the most economical. And it's easy to mix and match patterns with white chinaware for an interesting look.

Add to this setting wooden, silver or white ceramic candle holders with white candles and, in the center, a white pitcher, bowl or clear glass vase with white tulips, a few freesia stems, white roses or white lilacs. The greenery from the stems and leaves is all that's needed for a touch of color. Dress the sideboard (if you have one) with a white eyelet-edged runner. This is a common item found at flea markets, but you can find new, inexpensive items like this at bed and bath shops. If you rummage through your mother's or grandmother's linen drawer you may find something similar.

I collect napkins. They are inexpensive and provide color easily when I want to create a theme. For fall I use my rust-and-moss-green-plaid linen napkins on a brown tablecloth. During the holidays I have Christmas napkins in bright green and cherry-red checks. When I'm serving an Italian meal, I use my red-and-white-checked napkins, and sometimes I like a black-and-white theme. I have black napkins and candles that look great on a white tablecloth with my ornate silver candlesticks. Pale pink damask, blue and white stripes, beige and white checks, and a mix of pastel colors and floral patterns are included in my collection. When you have a variety of napkins and a few basic tablecloths or place mats, you can easily set a table to match your mood, a theme, the weather, the season or your meal. Try it. It's a lot of fun. .

Personal Touches

The dining room is a wonderful place to display collectibles and artwork. For example, a friend of mine travels each year to a different country and collects pottery wherever she goes. She had a shelf built high on the walls around the room where she displays her plates. A collection of baskets in an open cupboard will lend texture and character to a country dining room. A collection of blue-and-white willowware displayed in a china cabinet would echo the theme in a blue-and-white room. You might create a vignette of objects on a small table under a window. Arrange high and low items such as two candlesticks, a small plant in a pretty ceramic cachepot, an interesting little plate in colors that reflect the wall or fabric color, a table lamp and a photograph in a standing frame. A simple clear glass vase filled with fresh cut flowers and a collection of shells in a basket might be all you need on a small table or shelf.

When my husband and I were working on our book *Nantucket Style*, we photographed an artist's house that was built in the 1700s. There was a very narrow wall space in the dining room, next to the door, and she used this to create a photographic display. Here she had framed black-and-white family portraits in the same simple black frames and arranged them to fill the area. Large colorful portraits of these same family members filled the larger walls around the room.

Another artist friend displays a collection of souvenir English coronation tins in the dining room. They are housed on glass shelves in a display case mounted on the wall and illuminated with lighting within the box.

Decorative accessories don't have to be expensive to be interesting. Whatever appeals to you can be used to add decorative touches. Plants, fresh flowers and potted trees add style to any room. Flowering plants add color on windowsills. When in doubt, use white and garden green. The freshest and nicest color combination is a grouping of white flowering plants with deep green leaves in simple terra-cotta pots. Look for old, used garden pots at yard sales. Sometimes you can find interesting shapes. I like to whitewash mine or create a mixture of glaze and paint to rub over them, very crudely, to make them look Old World. Place these on ceramic dishes on a highly polished table. It's fun to mix textures and put things together that you wouldn't expect to find side by side.

online help
BHG Live
www.BHGLive.com
The *Better Homes and Gardens* group of magazines online. Links to *Ladies' Home Journal, Traditional Home, Midwest Living* and *Wood*. Includes previews of upcoming issues. It's all current, has lots of tips for decorating and is very well presented.

The Bedrooms

A bedroom should be the place where you go to unwind. It should be a totally relaxing environment. Whether your room is large or small, you can create your perfect dream bedroom. It might be a room done only in soft tones of white with absolutely no color. You might use furniture made of warm woods, such as honey-colored pine, with creamy white linens, lace-edged pillow cases and lace panels or white shutters at the windows, and white or beige wall-to-wall carpeting. Or you might prefer a blue-and-white theme with touches of yellow accents in the wallpaper. The bed linens and billowy balloon shades at the windows might be made from the same fabric to match the wallpaper and, underfoot, a deep blue carpet.

Everyone has a different idea of what a perfect bedroom would be, and it isn't difficult to achieve. You may not know what else you want, but you know you'll need a bed, so this is a good place to begin. Since the bed is the dominant feature of the room, you can concentrate on making it perfect. It's the star of the show. If you already own a bed, but you bought it several years ago, this might be a good time to buy a new one. Select the size that's right for you. A queen-size bed is luxurious for one and comfortable for two. For this reason it's the most popular size. Buy the very best mattress you can afford. It will last a long time and you will thank yourself every single night.

Aside from the bed, which includes the mattress, boxspring and frame, you'll want bed linens, pillows, side tables, dresser, maybe a small desk and chair, reading lamps, mirror and accessories such as art, framed photographs and collectibles.

Once you've conjured up your dream bedroom, you'll probably know the color scheme you like best. You have the option of painting, wallpapering, stenciling or applying a faux finish to the walls. Bedroom floors feel and look best when carpeted, but if you have wonderful wood floors, consider an area rug. The carpeting in this room should be plush and comfy. It should make you feel luxurious.

You can introduce color, texture and patterns with fabric on the bed, the dust ruffle around the bed, perhaps on a padded headboard, on cushions and pillows and on the windows if you decide to have curtains.

While your dream bedroom might be one filled with cabbage rose prints and a riot of color, I can't begin to overstate my feelings about bedrooms. They should be devoid of any harsh colors, patterns or textures, and the simpler and more luxurious the bedding, the better. For a while the trend was toward busy bedrooms with lots of frills and fluff. We're finally finding out that a pared-down room is easier on the body and soul, and more carefree. You can't know how restful you'll feel until you've ended your day in the sensuous surroundings of a soft-hued bedroom. It's like wrapping yourself in a warm cocoon of pampered bliss. We spend a lot of time in the bedroom, and this is where comfort counts the most.

Buying a Good Mattress

Last year we bought a new mattress and boxspring, which is the foundation on which the mattress rests. It was quite an event. My husband and I took our daughter, who was pregnant at the time, and our three-year-

Groucho Marx said, "Anything that can't be done in bed isn't worth doing at all."

old granddaughter to the store with us. We all tried out every mattress on the floor. Before making our selection, we had rolled, jumped, twisted and turned on soft, medium, hard, thick, thicker and thickest mattresses and even then it was hard to tell which would be the best. However, the Better Sleep Council in Washington, D.C., says this is the only way to buy a mattress. Try it out. This is not a job for the timid. No sitting on the edge and bouncing lightly up and down. Wear casual clothes and go to the store with your significant other and give those mattresses a good workout.

The Better Sleep Council further says that when you lie on your side, the mattress should feel comfortable. It should feel comfortable under your head, neck, shoulders, hips and knees. Lie on your back and slide your hand under the small of your back. The mattress should support you comfortably there. If you have back problems, look for a therapeutic mattress. If you have allergies, check the label for material contents.

Next, ask about warranties and life expectancy for the product in your price range. If a mattress is extremely comfortable and you find it costs more than you were prepared to spend, give up something else, but get the mattress that feels the best.

Quality is determined by the number of coils inside the mattress and the steel gauge. A top-of-the-line, queen-size bed, for example, will have as many as 700 coils. A good mattress has around 600. The more coils, the firmer the mattress. The mattress should also have two air holes on each side for air circulation.

The Plan

Before going any further with your decisions about wall, floor and window treatments, you should make a furniture placement plan. The position of the bed is the most important one. This is where you'll spend most of your time when you're in the bedroom.

If you know anything about the Eastern philosophy of feng shui, you know that the placement of furniture can bring harmony to every aspect of your life. Where better to employ this philosophy than in the bedroom? Supposedly, you can bring energy to your life as well as find inner peace just by placing your furniture in certain relationships to each other and the room. Rumor has it that even Donald Trump called in a feng shui adviser for one of his Manhattan buildings.

The main thrust of feng shui is that you can create an environment within your home that relates to the natural order of the universe. If you're curious, it can't hurt to consider some of the principles of this traditional Chinese school of thought. For example, concern with compass direction is important to feng shui practitioners. They profess that positioning your bed so that you can see the sun rise will do wonders for your morning attitude. Further, they suggest, never put your bed underneath a window; if possible, the head of the bed should face north or east, but should not be directly opposite the door.

Once you have the ideal aesthetic and spiritual location for the bed, the rest is easy. Night tables on each side should be large enough to hold your "stuff" and high enough to be comfortable. They don't have to match. In fact, you might use small dressers as side tables if you need extra storage and don't have room for a larger bureau. Or, use a small desk on one side of the bed with an occasional chair. If lamps aren't attached

Decorator Pat Giddings says, "Rooms with an abundance of curves are the most relaxing."

to the wall, they should be high enough for reading without shining in your eyes.

Decide where you will keep your clothes. It might be a dresser or armoire, but if you don't have enough room for another large piece of furniture, you can design and outfit your closet with shelves for efficient storage of bulky items. Once you've figured out where to put the essentials, you'll know how much room you have left for the extras.

Even a small, cast-off wooden chair is better than none in the bedroom. While you might be the neatest person in the world, you need a place to toss your clothes at night, or for holding a bathrobe or the laundry you don't have time to fold and put away. Find a corner to hold a charming little chair. This is an item that's easy to find, either old or new, for little money. If there's room for a comfortable easy chair or a chaise longue, all the better. Know your priorities and plan accordingly.

Other items that work well in a bedroom and don't take up much space are a quilt rack, a full-length mirror, a floor lamp and a television stand.

Color Notes

Colors have a strong impact on our moods. In a bedroom, you want to create a sense of calm, and your color scheme will help achieve this. Probably the most popular colors used in bedrooms are green and blue with white. Greens can help to create a restful ambience and are often used to impart serenity. Blues also suggest rest and calm if they aren't too dark. Intense shades of blue can be a nice accent in a neutral room.

Neutral colors are easy to live with and make good background colors. While gray is often used to create a neutral background color in other rooms, it's seldom used in a bedroom. Shades of brown and tan make a room warm and cozy, almost den-like.

White and near whites are always safe and you can introduce any color into the room. White walls tend to brighten up a room and make it look modern. Traditionally, doors, windows and room trims are painted white regardless of the other colors used in the room, but it isn't mandatory.

A Romantic Bedroom on a Shoestring

If you're on an incredibly tight budget, it's easy to create a romantic bedroom that looks like a million bucks. All it takes is a little time to search out some odd pieces of furniture with good lines, and a few cans of white paint. "Oh, sure!" you might exclaim. "Where will I find great furniture that doesn't cost an arm and a leg?" There is so much secondhand furniture around that once you start your search, you'll be amazed. We are not talking about antiques, just the kind of furniture that looks tired and dated. Don't turn down castoffs from relatives. Scour your parents' attic for forgotten or discarded furniture. They may have not-so-hidden, just overlooked

Actress and inveterate collector Teri Garr says about her approach to decorating: "I never throw anything away."

potential. These are the very pieces that, once given a new lease on life via nothing more than a few coats of plain white paint, can look sensational. A dark and scratched mahogany night table, for example, may not be appreciated because you're not looking beyond its ugly surface. If it has a nice shape and interesting lines, a coat or two of white paint will reveal its inherent beauty. Do this with all your mismatched wooden pieces and you'll have what it takes to create a room with more charm and character than one filled with store-bought furniture. Add to this some simply tossed or tacked-up vintage linens and your bedroom will look artfully put together.

The Best-Dressed Beds

No matter what style bed frame you choose, nothing is more important than what you put on the bed. Many famous designers are passionate about their beds, and when it comes to giving advice about bedding they border on the fanatic. No other question elicits such a unanimously enthusiastic response than asking a group of decorators to describe the basic elements for a heavenly bed. There's no question about it, sleeping in monklike fashion is definitely out, if it was ever in. Everyone agrees a bed should look so cozy and inviting that you can't wait to climb in.

When it comes to sheets, most prefer white or ivory fine-thread cotton. Linen represents the only alternative. For years I have held onto the fine white cotton sheets that once belonged to my mother because they are softer than any I could possibly buy. After years of washing they are as fine as silk. Nothing makes a bed more exquisite than perfectly ironed sheets. A down comforter in a white cotton or linen duvet in a summer and winter weight is a must, and if lots of pillows and a

When buying sheets, keep in mind that the higher the thread count (number of threads per square inch), the finer the feel. Specialty shops carry sheets with a 350 count, whereas your average cotton sheet has 200–250.

One hundred percent cotton sheets wrinkle, but they're softer than polyester, which dries more quickly and doesn't wrinkle.

Percale sheets have a thread count of 180 or more. Pima or Egyptian cotton is extra soft.

Never store linens in plastic as it will discolor them.

Protect pillows with a zippered cover that can be removed and washed. Air down pillows in the sun.

lace coverlet is your idea of heaven, add a folded patchwork quilt across the bottom of the bed for a winning combination.

Designer Paloma Picasso uses a light cotton quilt in the summer and wool blankets in the winter because she likes the weight and their substantial feel. Paris designer Andrée Putman collects thin white pique bed covers and favors the heavy linen sheets she found at a Toulouse flea market years ago.

No respectable bed gets four stars without lots of pillows, preferably covered in antique, embroidered cases, but not for the ones you sleep on. The finer the quality of the down, the more luxurious the bed looks. Two large, square European pillows in white mattelasse or vintage embroidered shams are perfect for sitting and reading in bed. Ideally, you can follow these with two firm feather pillows and two down ones. A couple of small pillows are good for tucking in where you need them if you spend a lot of time in bed. When the bed is made, the bevy of pillows makes it look great.

Wallpaper

A wallpaper treatment is often used to create an environment in the bedroom. It's a great way to change the look of the room with relatively little cost and time. Wallpapering is an easy do-it-yourself project, even if you've never done it before. (See page 223 for complete directions.) Another option is to wallpaper the ceiling as well, but this isn't a job for the novice.

When looking through sample books, you'll find that many wallpaper designs offer matching fabric. If you can make your own curtains, pillow covers, duvet and bed skirt, this is a good way to save money and personalize your room. Many pattern companies such as

Butterick, Vogue and McCall's offer patterns for making a complete bedroom ensemble.

Choose a wallpaper pattern in a color and design that you love. You don't have to be limited by one design. An overall floral pattern, for example, might have a matching border design to use around the top of the room. Take home the sample book and keep it around for a while to see if, after a few days, you still love the pattern you chose. Sometimes finding a wallpaper pattern that appeals to you can dictate a design direction. If you're in a quandary over what to do, go to a wallcovering store and browse through a few sample books for inspiration. Almost every pattern comes in several different colors. Wallpaper also varies in price range and quality. Get familiar with the products before making a final selection. Measure your room and bring the measurements to the store and the staff will figure out how many rolls you'll need.

If you're planning to do the wallpapering yourself, use prepasted paper. You simply wet the back to apply it directly to the wall. No paste is needed. Avoid striped patterns as they are more difficult to match from strip to strip, and if your walls are not perfectly straight it's hard to do a perfect job. A small, repeating overall pattern is the easiest to work with, or one that is quite large. All the wallpapering equipment you'll need is available at a home center. The materials are few and inexpensive.

For a quick and easy wallpaper treatment, rolls of self-stick borders are now available in a wide variety of patterns and styles.

Floors

For bedroom floors, wall-to-wall carpeting has no rival. If you don't want to cover the floor completely, consider an area rug or a few scatter rugs. A painted floor is another option. Decorative painting techniques include spattering, combing, sponging or stenciling. (See page 219 for how-to's.) A popular design is the two-color checkerboard pattern of painted alternating light and dark squares across the floor, in a size appropriate to the room.

Carpeting warms up a room, adds color and deadens sound. Carpeting comes in thousands of patterns, colors and styles for every budget. If you have pattern in the room, such as on the bed, curtains or walls, solid-color carpeting is best. Since this isn't a high-traffic area, you can go for looks over practicality.

Before shopping for a carpet, measure the room accurately. Then go to a reputable dealer who knows his or her trade. The dealer will be able to advise you on the best product within your price range. Ask if there's a charge for installation and factor in the cost of an underlay. Take samples home to check them out in the room, in natural and artificial light. Most carpets today are low maintenance, with stain, odor and static resistance.

A good carpet style for bedrooms is Saxony plush. It's level cut with soft, deep pile. With a dense pad underneath, it is luxurious. Berber carpets are another favorite, especially in a neutral room. They're made of tweedy, heathered yarns and wear well. Sisal is another option for neutral rooms, and this practical material has long been the choice of decorators for any area of the house, including stairways. It's not as luxurious in feeling as a plush carpet, but it's handsome, classic and low in maintenance. If you're interested, check out differ-

Drysdale Design Associates thinks floors are more important than walls. Its advice: "A border can be used to frame a rug and smooth the transition from floor to walls."

ent kinds of sisal, as there are varying degrees of coarseness, and for a bedroom you want a fiber that feels good under bare feet.

Windows

Generally speaking, bedroom windows need some covering for privacy and light control. You have the options of shades, blinds, shutters, curtains or drapes. Many bedrooms have dormer windows, which require special attention. A decorator I know had four dormer windows in her bedroom. She wallpapered inside these charming niches and hung simple lace panels on brass rods across the panes.

Curtains to Match Your Style

Choose the window treatment that reflects the style of the room. For example, for a traditional bedroom you might hang pinch-pleated chintz or linen panels from the top of the window molding to the floor. For a formal bedroom, consider graceful balloon shades or full-length tiebacks with a valance to finish off the top. If the bedroom has a large wall expanse of windows, plain draperies that can easily be drawn closed on a track with a valanced top would be a good choice. For a country look, consider shutters or café curtains. If a sleek, contemporary look is what you're after, miniblinds, wooden blinds or fabric shades would look good. Lace panels are perfect for a romantic, all-white bedroom. You can purchase them in a size to suit your window, and they already have holes for the rod.

Sheer panels allow light to come through and give some degree of privacy. They are always fresh-looking and, if you have standard windows, you can get inex-

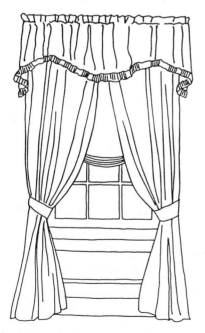

Floor-to-ceiling tieback curtains with custom shade and valance

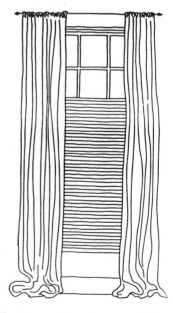

Floor-to-ceiling sheer curtains with bottom-mounted privacy blinds

132

pensive ready-mades. Even if they're too long, it's easy to hem them or better yet, allow them to "puddle" onto the floor. Hang sheer curtains on a brass rod with the fabric loosely gathered and held back gracefully on decorative finials at the sides of the windows. Install plain shades behind them for privacy. Many mail-order home catalogs sell ready-made curtains that have a custom-made look. Choose an interesting rod and finials to give them a personal touch.

Perhaps your window only needs a valance or swag of fabric to soften and frame the view. A tall window benefits from a swag or jabot that goes across the top and borders the sides of the windows in gentle folds. A valance caps off the top of a window and, if the fabric matches or corresponds to the colors or pattern in the wallpaper or furniture, it creates a nice finishing detail. Treat a double set or bay of windows as one. This area might be able to accommodate a lavish treatment such as wide tieback draperies and a deep valance that extends beyond the window frames on each side.

Cheap Solution

If you want an instant window treatment that will look good and cost little, use sheets. Sheets come in a variety of sizes, colors and patterns, and the least expensive—polyester—are best because they are stiff and hold a nice shape. Choose a design with a decorative border that will become the header or the bottom hem on your curtain. Open each side of the top or bottom hem (depending on which way you want to hang it) to create a channel for threading onto the rod. If you buy an extra single sheet to match, you can cut off the border, leaving a little extra strip of the sheet for finishing off the edge, and use this to make tiebacks for the panel curtains.

For another inexpensive solution, buy plain white

panels (or use sheets) and add your own decorative trim for a custom look. This might be a strip of grosgrain or velvet ribbon stitched down the edges, braid or gimp, a border stencil design, or a border made from printed fabric.

Interesting tiebacks add detail to plain curtains and they're easy to make. Or buy colorful silk cording and attach tassels to the ends. These and all sorts of trimmings are available at sewing and fabric shops. A popular decorating trick is to make a simple tieback from 6-inch-wide French taffeta ribbon with wired edges tied in a luxurious bow at each side. Hold them in place with cup hooks attached to the window frames. Or stencil a strip of fabric and make it into a tieback.

When tying back the curtains, experiment until you like the positioning and the amount of fabric coverage on the windows. Tie the curtains back loosely so the curve or billow of the fabric hangs gracefully. Try it at different heights before attaching it permanently.

Furniture

The furnishings in the bedroom can be whatever makes you comfortable. There are no rules. Think about what you'll need most and the space you have for each item. Once the bed is in position, you'll know if you have room on each side for night tables, or if you only have room for one. Look for dead space that can be used for storage. A trunk at the end of the bed, for example, can be used for holding an extra blanket as well as bulky sweaters and out-of-season clothes. If you need to conserve space, you might be able to fit a low dresser in the closet with room above for hanging short items and space on one side for longer items.

It's important to know how you will use your bedroom. Some people like to watch television in bed; oth-

Tip
Anything you use every day should be high quality. Buy the best mattress you can afford even if you have to store your clothes in cardboard boxes for a year.

ers want a comfortable chair and reading lamp. Perhaps you enjoy lounging in the bedroom, in which case a chaise longue, love seat or armchair and ottoman will fill the bill. A standing lamp next to the chaise or chair could eliminate the need for a small table if there isn't enough room for one.

If you like the warm feeling created by displaying lots of knickknacks, plan space for a shelving unit or wall shelves for holding picture frames, vases and other objects of art.

Once you have your list of "must haves" in order of importance, you can begin to plan where each will fit into the room. If something has to go, it should be the item you can most easily live without. If you want it all, you may have to look for smaller-scale items in order to find inches here and there. A full-size bed, for example, might replace the queen, and a highboy dresser might replace a double bureau. The right bed and a bureau for holding clothes are the most important items. Plan these first, then add.

Beds

Don't buy a bed in haste. It's too important a purchase to make it lightly. Take time to decide what size will be the most comfortable for you, whether you sleep alone or with a significant other. Another consideration is height. How high off the floor do you want the bed to be? This is difficult to decide before going to a showroom and trying out different styles to see how it feels to sit on the side of the bed or getting on and off.

Don't let anyone convince you that a bed frame is unimportant. This is the headboard and footboard and side rails, not the metal frame that mattress stores provide. A headboard is an important design element, but it's also practical. Where else could you lean pillows and sit up to read?

Aside from modern designs, you'll find both reproductions and originals of Early American and European styles in a wide variety of woods. For example, the sleigh bed, with identical, generously curved headboard

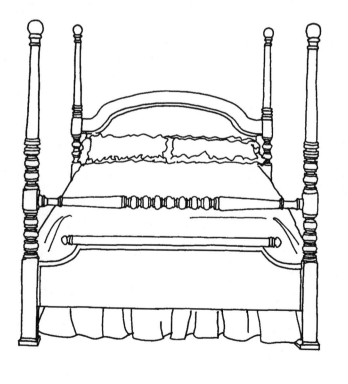

and footboard, originated in the early 1800s and was made by cabinetmakers in every city from the east coast to the Mississippi. Traditional four-posters, canopies, eighteenth-century pencil posts and brass and iron beds are just some of your options.

Another option is a soft, slipcovered headboard. This is usually a sturdy frame comfortably padded and upholstered in a fabric of your choice. Mail-order catalogs often offer uncovered headboards made of particle board for the do-it-yourselfer. If you can sew, it's easy to cover the headboard with quilt batting and stitch up the slipcover. This is a good way to save money.

Armoires

Armoires and freestanding closets offer other options for storing clothes. These rather large pieces of furniture usually have two or four doors on the front. The interior design determines how it's used. One style has a simple clothes rod; another has a clothes rod across the top half with two pullout drawers beneath. Some are quite elaborate, outfitted with lingerie drawers as well as being mirrored on the inside of the doors.

An armoire called an entertainment cabinet is designed with open shelves that are large and deep enough to accommodate a television set and VCR as well as stereo equipment. There are predrilled holes for wires in the back and drawers for storage. It's a good solution for concealing electronics in the bedroom.

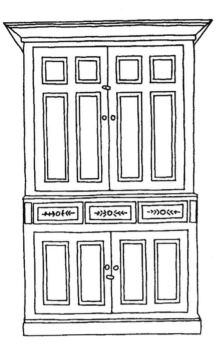

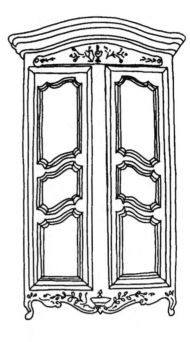

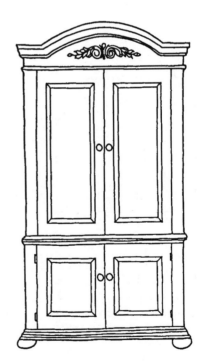

Dressers and Dressing Tables

When choosing a dresser, think about what will go into it. Decide if you need fewer, thus larger drawers, small drawers, or a combination of both. A chest of drawers can accommodate everything from socks to bulky sweaters. If you don't want to spend a lot of money, an old bureau of any sort, even an old record cabinet, can be stripped, stained or painted to use for holding clothes. Unfurnished furniture stores have all sizes of bureaus, chests of drawers, lingerie chests and night stands with drawers in a variety of styles including period reproductions.

If you have limited counter space in the bathroom, use a dressing table in the bedroom to hold toiletries. It provides a place to apply makeup as well as a surface for displaying pretty accessories. Many dressing tables have a shallow drawer for holding odds and ends. Some can accommodate a fabric skirt around the rim, making it possible to store bulky items underneath.

Mirrors

If a mirror is mounted on the wall above the dresser, its size should relate to the size of the furniture. I prefer a full-length mirror in the bedroom and the bathroom. If you can find an old one in an ornate or interesting frame, this can be hung as a piece of art. Old frames are easy to find at junk shops and even easier to refinish with paint or stain. If you find an interesting frame, take it to a hardware store and have a mirror cut to fit. This is not costly. Dressing mirrors sit on top of a dressing table or bureau. A cheval mirror is one that swivels in a frame and sits on the floor. These are sometimes available in unfinished furniture stores and you might stain or paint the frame in a color to go with the furnishings in the room.

Lighting

Lighting in the bedroom has two purposes, for ambience, and for reading or other tasks. If it's possible to have your bedroom lighting on a dimmer control, this will give you flexibility. Bedside lamps should be high enough to read by, but if you want soft lighting some of the time, a lamp that takes a three-way bulb is a good idea.

Wall-mounted, adjustable swing-arm lamps are often used on either side of a bed. They are available in many styles and can be mounted on the wall exactly where the lighting is most comfortable. This type of lamp leaves the night table next to the bed free for other items.

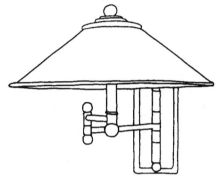

There are times when you want soft, romantic lighting in the room, just a whisper above darkness, and not the glow from the television set. A small boudoir lamp that takes a low wattage bulb, even a pink bulb, might sit on a dresser or desk. Make sure the bottom of the shade is below eye level so it doesn't shine in your eyes when you're in bed.

Lamp Shades

The size and style of the lamp will determine the shade. A translucent shade is best when you want a soft lighting effect. For good reading you want an opaque shade because the light will be concentrated downward.

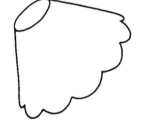

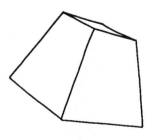

Accessories

Artwork and accessories are added after the room is complete. The term *accessories* refers to decorative objects that add to the overall ambience of the room. These are usually small objects such as vases, clocks, figurines, crafts, framed photographs and collectibles that can be changed at will. They can be antiques or modern objects, and they don't have to match the style or period of the room.

Accessories give a room personality and make it looked lived in. Introducing things that are personal makes the room look charming and interesting. Personal family photographs belong in the bedroom, and you can hang them on the walls or make a grouping on a table, desk or bookshelf. I have an antique night table that I painted white and use for a display in one corner of the room. I placed a vintage lace-edged tea cloth on the diagonal over the table; then I made a grouping with my favorite snapshots in different sizes and types of frames.

When in Doubt

After you've arranged a few things, take something away, then add something else. Keep doing this until you have a look that pleases you. If you aren't sure what looks good where, remember it's not such an important decision. A vase of flowers on a night stand, a stack of two or three books, a pretty plate to hold incidentals at the end of the day and a framed botanical print on the wall are all you need to give a room your spin.

The accessories will find their way into your home. Once you are in the decorating mode, you'll see things as never before. Suddenly weekend yard sales and antique browsing will take on a whole new meaning. The incidentals your mother or grandmother tried to foist on you will take on heirloom proportions if you have a

Tip
If you make a mistake, correct it as soon as possible and get on with the decorating process. Working around an uncorrected mistake will influence every decision you make from that point on.

bare table that cries out for something personal from your past. A collection of shells, old toys, a fishing trophy, a framed graduation certificate or even a basket of colorful yarn may be just what you need to create an interesting display in your new home.

Storage

Nobody ever has enough storage. No matter what size your closet is, you can make the most of it if you plan carefully. Closet systems such as the coated wire shelves sold at home centers provide a wonderful solution for any situation. They are designed so you can create a closet to accommodate your specific needs. Another way to add closet space is to hang a second rod below the original one. You'll be able to hang twice the number of shirts, pants and jackets.

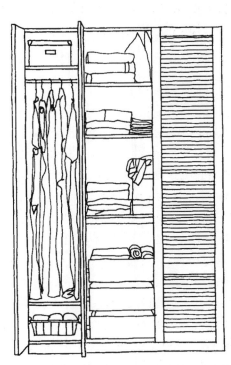

Aside from installing shelves in the closet, there are inexpensive storage solutions for just about anything you want to put away. Several specialty mail-order catalogs and stores are devoted to making your life incredibly organized.

Bookcases offer storage space for certain items that fit neatly onto narrow shelves. For example, use plastic sweater boxes, hat boxes or baskets to hold underwear, scarves and socks on shelves.

Place a divider screen across a dead corner of the room to conceal a clothes tree, a large wicker hamper, plastic milk crates for holding shoes or sweats, or an ugly dresser. Attach hooks to the back of the screen for hanging clothes. Building in shelves around a window might be the perfect way to create an interesting display area, as well as adding architectural interest to

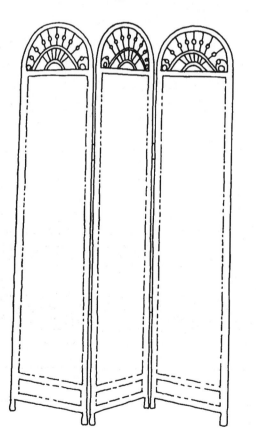

the room. A window seat with a lift-up top is another building project that can be good-looking and practical. If building even a small project isn't in the plan, consider a trunk. If it has a flat top, like a toy box, for example, it can also be used as a bench at the end of the bed or under a window. A fabric-covered foam cushion and a loose pillow would make this item ideal for sitting and storing.

Cover an inexpensive, round composition board table (they come in various sizes) with a quilt, full length table cover or a blanket, topped with a lovely linen square. Use this as a night table on one side of the bed; the concealed area under the table is perfect for unsightly storage. The top will hold much more than an ordinary-size end table and it will look quite elegant.

Office supply catalogs and art stores can be great sources for storage units that might not be obvious for use in a bedroom. For example, a little taboret unit on rollers called a "Boby" is used in art studios. The drawers swing out and there are shelves and all sorts of storage space packed neatly into the 18- x 18-inch unit. It's extremely versatile and compact. Hobbyists have discovered it for sewing equipment and other tools, but it can be used in the bedroom or stored inside a closet.

Looking Up and Down

There's always room at the top. Run a deep shelf across one entire wall of the room, as high as you can comfortably reach. Line the shelf with laundry baskets or other good-looking large containers for storage. They should all be identical in order not to look messy or cluttered. Add a shelf above the door for holding books or collectibles.

Don't forget the area under the bed. Keeping in mind the height of the frame, find cardboard storage boxes to hold out-of-season clothes. Custom bed frames and even high-end box springs made by Slumberland come equipped with a deep drawer. Consider purchasing such a bed if space and storage are limited.

The things you use the least—out-of-season clothes, extra blankets, old tax records, and memorabilia you want to save but not necessarily display—should be the least accessible. If they are put away in boxes under the bed or on a top shelf of the closet, be sure to label the outside, as most people tend to forget what is out of sight. Plastic storage containers can eliminate a lot of guesswork if you want to know at a glance what you're storing.

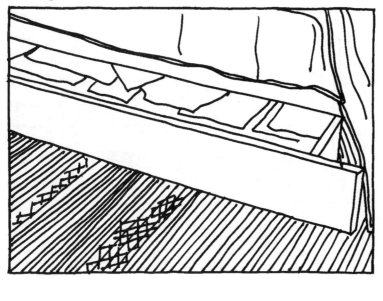

Modular Units

It's easy to build a wall of storage with identical-size cubes. These units are sold separately so you can create your own custom storage system to fit anywhere. A tall, narrow tower of shelves, for example, can stand alone or become the basis for an entire wall of storage. You will also find cubes that hold adjustable shelves and vertical dividers. Whether you need storage space to hold your media equipment or clothes, a modular shelving unit makes sense and can be quite attractive. An entire wall unit filled with books would be practical as well as good-looking.

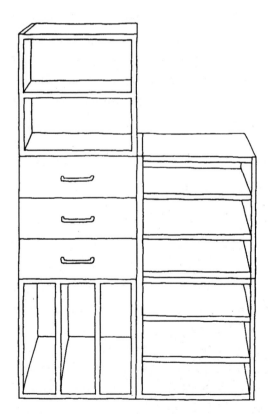

Rooms for Children

If you're decorating a room to be used as a nursery, keep in mind that babies grow quickly into toddlers, who grow into preschoolers, who grow into school age children, and all along the way the room must change to meet their growing needs. While it's tempting to decorate the perfect nursery, aside from the crib, think about furniture that can grow with the child.

Your child will be in a crib for as long as you can possibly keep him or her there. This means he or she will either climb out around age two and you will know that it's time for a bed, or will graduate to a bed with a side guard because the crib is needed for a new sibling. So you have a short time to enjoy a frilly nursery, but the goal should be to design a room that's flexible. As children grow beyond the infant stage, their bedrooms become more than a place to sleep. This is where they play, read and possibly fingerpaint. Nothing in this room should be untouchable or unwashable. Everything should be safe, carefree and sturdy. You'll also need to plan for good storage of clothing as well as the abundance of paraphernalia that will ultimately accumulate.

A Working Plan

Good storage space is the most important thing for making a baby's room function well. There has to be a place for clothes, toys and equipment. The basic furniture includes a crib, later to be replaced with a bed, a changing table and a dresser. Shelving units that can be added to and moved up and down are essential. When my daughter had her first baby she purchased a modular storage unit with equal-size open cubes that could be arranged in many different ways and could also be added to. In this way she could build a unit as high and as wide as she wanted. When her son was four, she arranged one row of cubes on top of another along one wall. Her preschooler uses the cubbies for his toys, and the top surfaces are just the right height on which to play with his cars. These cubes are available through discount stores and mail-order catalogs.

Safety First

Safety is your primary concern. New cribs have safety standards, so don't accept your old crib from your parents for sentimental reasons, even if it's in perfect condition. It was probably painted before lead testing and the slats undoubtedly are further apart than today's required standard.

Furniture should not tip over easily and everything should be rounded rather than made with sharp edges. Functional furniture made from easy-to-clean materials like laminates are practical choices.

Furniture That Grows Up

When buying storage units, consider unfinished dressers that you can paint in a color to go with the scheme you've chosen. These items can be outfitted with over-sized round knobs, modern drawer pulls or fanciful knobs sold in home centers. If you buy two small dressers rather than one large one, they can be placed side by side to look like one large bureau. However, when the child is older you can separate the dressers in order to create a space wide enough for a chair and have a board cut to fit across the entire expanse, thus creating a desk or work surface. If you paint the dressers in a pastel or white for the baby, they can easily be repainted in a bright color for an older child.

Shelves running around a room can hold stuffed animals and decorative items as well as diapers and changing equipment. Later, these shelves will serve to hold books and other toys. A toy box will last from nursery to school age and can be decorated with a wallpaper border in a nursery theme and later painted or repapered for an older child. Look for the type that has a safety hinge. This means that when the lid is lifted it

won't slam down on little fingers. It stays in whatever position it's lifted to.

Another essential item for the nursery is a rocking chair. It should have a padded cushion on the seat and back. A footstool will give you added comfort when feeding and rocking the baby. A little pillow to fit in the small of your back and one for under the arm that cradles the baby's head while feeding is a necessity. At about the same time you replace the crib with a bed, you'll probably replace the rocker with a child-size table and chairs if you don't have room for both.

Baskets are helpful for quick pickups of baby clothes and to hold extra blankets and diapers. Later they are wonderful containers for organizing toys. Laundry baskets are perfect for holding toy trucks and cars and can be shoved into the closet at day's end.

Color

Children respond to bright colors. Even if the walls are white or pale pastel you can add bright accents on window and door trims, furniture, rugs and painted modular storage units. For a soft theme, paint the walls pale yellow. This is a good, safe color for a boy or girl. You can then add accents in sherbet colors like pistachio and melon for the curtains and crib set. If the floor isn't in good condition, paint it a light color and apply a spatter paint treatment using a variety of pastel colors. This is a practical way to treat the floors in a child's room. Deck or yacht paint is sold specially for floors.

If you want a bright color scheme, you can't go wrong with shiny paint in primary colors on the walls and furniture. Be sure that the paint you use is lead free. Color can be added with wallpaper, and you'll find designs in every conceivable theme, from favorite Disney characters to bicycles racing around a border. All the Beatrix Potter characters and illustrations are represented in wallpaper designs as well, if this is your idea of the perfect nursery theme.

If saving money is key, apply a fanciful stencil to the walls. This is a great way to express yourself and create a delightful room with a simple or extremely lavish design. It's easy and the design can be painted over when it is no longer suitable. A wide variety of pre-cut stencils and materials are available in all craft and art supply stores.

Aside from stencils, there are kits consisting of die-cut images, much like Colorforms, that you simply press onto the walls. The elements are provided for creating your own wall border or an entire scene in a variety of themes, such as animals, rainbows, flowers or cartoon characters. When you want to remove them, just peel them away. They leave no marks on the wall. The 3M

Tip
Use color in unexpected places. For example, paint the inside of a closet a bright color.

Company makes an extensive line of wall decorations in kits that include a wide border strip long enough to go around an average-size room, and all the decorating elements. For example, the border for a zoo theme will include a colorful background strip representing a zoo-like environment and kangaroos, elephants, zebras, monkeys and more that can be placed anywhere on the border as well as here and there on the wall.

Instant Wall Decor

No paste, no water, no backing paper, no mess. If this appeals to you, it's possible to get self-adhesive wallpaper borders that go straight from the roll onto the wall. You'll find decorative motifs from childlike nursery designs to sophisticated florals and geometrics. For older children there are dolphins, brightly colored stylized animals, realistic safari animals, tropical fish, carousels, planes and trains and autos. Just measure the strips to go along a wall and press into place. You can decorate the room in less than an hour.

Windows

Aside from looking good, a window treatment should allow for light and air circulation and provide a way to darken the room. Long curtains are impractical. A crawling baby will head straight for them. Café curtains, shades or blinds are best. Keep the treatment simple and carefree. Shades are the most practical and come in a wide range of colors and designs. If you use a shade you can add a fabric valance or a café curtain and valance to match the colors in the room or the fabric on the crib or bed. You can customize plain shades with a painted or stenciled design, or apply press-on designs from a room decorating kit to match the wall decor.

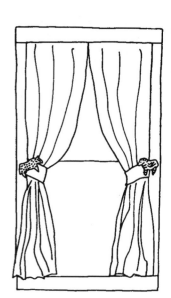

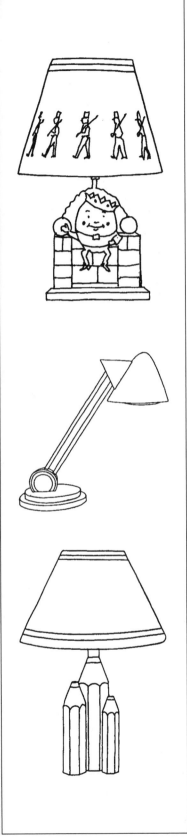

Floors

From the time they start to sit up and crawl, children spend a lot of time on the floor. The floor should be warm, uncluttered, safe and easy to clean. If it's nonslip and not hard this is a plus, especially in the early years when kids haven't quite gotten their balance. Resilience and soundproofing are other considerations. Remember, too, that the floor is the surface for a young child's play and should be smooth enough to run cars and toys over easily. In the end, the choice boils down to a carpeted surface or a bare one.

Vinyl flooring is practical because it's durable and easy to clean, and it's softer than a wood floor. A small area carpet could be placed in front of the crib or under your feet in front of the rocker for warmth. If you opt for carpeting it should be made of a low-pile fiber for high-traffic areas, and be stain and static resistant.

Lighting

You'll want two types of lighting in a nursery. In general, you'll want the lighting to be soft and diffused, but you'll also need task lighting over the changing table. For an older child's room, you'll still need the soft lighting since young children often want a light left on at night, but you'll need bright lights for their play and work areas.

If you have overhead lighting, a dimmer switch is a good thing to install. It's inexpensive and will give you the lighting control you need for different situations. You'll also need a night light. There are many novelty lamps that are actually decorative night lights and that sit on a table or dresser, not the kind you insert directly into the electrical outlet. You can use a low-wattage bulb in any type of table lamp.

Do-It-Yourself Motifs

1. Animals are a good starting point for the nursery. Stencil them on the wall as a border, on the front of dresser drawers, on the panels of the closet door and on a toy box.

2. It's easy to paint a simple border around the room. Measure down from the ceiling approximately 6 to 8 inches and run a strip of painter's tape (unlike masking tape, it won't pull the paint off the wall when you peel the tape away) along the wall as a guideline. Paint the border sky blue. Let it dry. Stencil yellow stars and moon shapes at random on top of the blue border. Use this color scheme for sheets, bumpers and a quilt on the crib, window treatment and floor covering. Paint the dresser with the same blue paint and add yellow stars and moons to the drawer fronts.

3. Use the simple stencil design of a car to create a border design around a toddler's room. Position the border halfway up the wall. Use a strip of painter's tape to delineate a line above which you'll stencil the design. Use bright blue and red paint colors and alternate for each car.

4. Paint the bottom half of the walls with a soft pastel color. Then add a wallpaper border around the room as high as a chair rail. Apply a wallpaper with a soft over-all pattern on the top half of the wall.

5. For a quick and easy design, paint the room a solid color, then apply a wallpaper border around the windows and doors.

6. For a coordinated look, use a matching crib bumper, sheets, crib skirt, quilt and curtains. Paint the walls and furniture one of the colors in the fabric.

7. If the rest of your home is decorated in a country style, carry the theme into the nursery. Use transparent deck stain, such as Thompson's Water Seal stains, in one of over a hundred colors on unfinished furniture. Let dry and apply a coat of satin polyurethane to protect the finish. Or whitewash the furniture with a coat of white latex paint. Let dry for a few minutes, then wipe away the excess to allow the natural wood to show through. Let dry overnight and coat with polyurethane.

8. Revive old wicker furniture with a coat of spray paint. A wicker chair, a small night table and a dresser will combine to create a charming and romantic baby's room. Add eyelet trim, ribbon or rickrack to the edge of café curtains and a valance.

9. It's easy to create a room of cloudlike softness with sponge-painted walls in a pastel blue, pink or yellow. Begin by painting the walls with a light color latex paint. Then, using a natural sponge, dip it into white latex paint, remove the excess on newsprint and, working on one small area at a time, pounce the sponge over the dry painted wall. Continue to do this until you've achieved a subtle, textured effect. If there is too much contrast, just keep going over the area until it looks good to you. This technique is absolutely foolproof. Cover the entire wall with random sponging in this way. You can use this technique on furniture as well. The goal is for a blending of colors that are closely related in shading. It's not advisable to use a light and dark color together as the results will be harsh.

10. If sponging walls isn't your thing, but you like a faux finished effect, you can get any treatment you like in wallpaper. It is so real looking that no one will guess it's not the real thing.

Rooms for Guests

I sleep in the guest bedroom in my house once a year. I do this to assess the room for comfort and to add whatever's necessary before inviting guests to stay with me. You can have fun with a guest bedroom because it probably won't be used as much as the other rooms. Therefore, you can get away with decorating touches that aren't entirely practical on an everyday basis. However, if you don't have the luxury of an extra room, chances are your guests will be sleeping on a pull-out sleep sofa in the den or home office.

Creating a stylish room for dual purposes can present an interesting challenge.

Since I live in a resort area, I'm usually prepared for a few guests during the summer months. The room

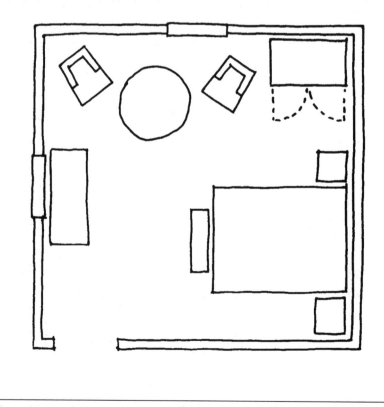

doesn't get used much in the winter so I decorated it in a summery way. I can always add a down comforter and quilt to the bed for winter use if necessary. Friends of mine decorated a den/study for optimum use every day, and for their occasional weekend guests. While my guest room is outfitted in white eyelet, theirs is furnished in tweeds, leather, chrome and glass. One wall is a built-in bookcase, there is a small TV, and most of the time the room is a sleek but cozy den. The floor is carpeted, there are wood blinds on the windows, and the tailored sofa opens into a queen-size bed. Small glass-and-chrome tables function as coffee tables in front of the sofa and, when pulled to each side, become night tables for guests. Two occasional chairs complete the den, and are easily

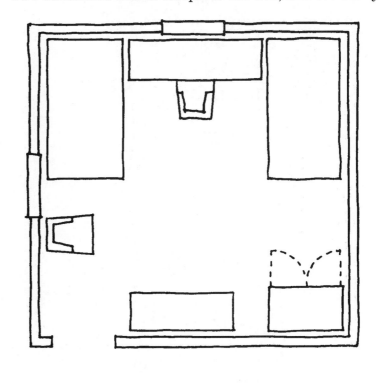

pushed out of the way when the sofa is opened up.

A friend who often has weekend guests suggests twin beds pushed together because this arrangement accommodates any situation. My guest bedroom has a double bed because the room would be too small for night tables on either side if the bed was larger. A double bed is a bit small for two, but most guests stay only two nights, so it isn't too uncomfortable. It's fine for one.

Where your guests sleep isn't as important as how you accommodate them, whether with twin beds tucked under eaves in an attic space, a futon in a tiny space, a sleep sofa in your office or a sumptuous bed in a beautifully decorated bedroom. Wherever your guests sleep, the room should be attractive and function well. Most of all it should be inviting. When your guests close the door to their temporary home, they should feel at home.

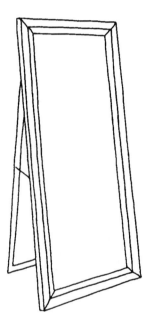

Guest Checklist

No matter how small, a guest bedroom can be comfortable if you do the following:

1. Remove all of your personal items. A guest room shouldn't be the catchall for last year's Christmas wrapping paper with closets full of old clothes that you've probably forgotten.

2. Line dresser drawers with scented paper. Fill the closet with pretty hangers.

3. The bed, no matter how it evolves, must be comfortable. Try it out yourself before having guests use it. A quilted mattress pad, pretty sheets, a blanket and comforter make the bed inviting. A patchwork or appliqué quilt adds to the homey quality.

4. Lots of pillows, soft and firm, will be appreciated.

5. Keep the furnishings simple. This is not the place to store castoffs so your guests have to navigate through the room. A night table and reading lamps, a small dresser and a chair are enough. If there's room, a bench at the end of the bed is good for sitting and holding a suitcase. I keep a wicker trunk at the end of my guest bed. It holds all the bed linens and towels, and guests use this for their suitcases.

6. Accessories that add to the comfort include a mirror (full-length if possible), clock and phone.

7. Fresh flowers, current magazines, a local newspaper and books make guests feel welcome. Pots of flowering plants on a shelf or windowsill add color and liveliness.

Good Furniture Buys

You might not want to spend a lot of money furnishing a den or a guest room. Once you buy a good bed or pull-out sofa, consider unfinished or secondhand furniture for the other pieces. Unfinished furniture has come a long way. But, like other furniture, some is of better quality than others. This means they are constructed well and well designed. For example, if Shaker style is appealing to you, you can find some very nice, ready-to-finish furniture with these classic straight lines. If a formal or traditional room is more to your liking, you'll find period furniture as well in every price range. When painted, stained or faux finished, this furniture can be quite outstanding for a fraction of what a finished piece might cost. If you go this route for the basic hard pieces such as a dresser, end tables, a coffee table, a wall storage unit, an entertainment center, a chair or an armoire, you can fill in with interesting finds along the way. Introducing a few good pieces will elevate the painted furniture for an interesting eclectic look.

Inexpensive wicker furniture is widely available in places like Pier 1 Imports and discount stores. It's great for an extra room because it's light and movable. It can also do double duty. For example, two wicker chairs with seat cushions, a coffee table and end tables will look just as good in a bedroom, a den or a porch. A wicker trunk can be outfitted with a glass top and serve as a coffee or end table, and it's perfect for storage if space is tight. It's also easy to spray paint wicker in a color of your choice.

Cardboard dressers, used primarily for storing off-season clothes and not meant for everyday use, can be terrific for a guest room. Modular cubes made of particle board can be painted, covered with contact paper, wallpaper or fabric, and arranged to hold sweaters, shoes and small items. The top becomes a surface on which to place a lamp, clock and other incidentals. Two cubes, one on top of the other, on each side of the bed create a comfortable height for night tables. You'll find them in home centers and discount catalogs.

Director's chairs with brightly colored canvas seats to match the room decor solve a space problem. They are comfortable and can easily be folded away when not needed. Perhaps this is why, after all these years, they are still so popular.

Accessories

Accessories can give a room warmth and character and you'll find just what you want at a price you can afford. For example, quilts are now quite reasonable and are wonderful for use on beds, over a sofa or as a wall hanging. Buy an inexpensive round table made of composition board and cover it with a pretty patchwork quilt that reaches the floor. Use this as an end table or next to a chair in your guest room or den. Add a small lamp for reading and a few pretty accessories.

Pillows are easy to make or inexpensive to buy in just the right style and fabric for all uses. In fact, this is one of the best ways to change the look of a room whenever you want. Look for remnants of expensive brocade, needlepoint, silk or moire fabrics to make pillows for a den sofa. Since you'll need a small amount it won't cost much. Throw pillows for a sofa should be no smaller than 18 inches, and 20 to 22 is even better. Look for interesting trimming like silk cording or fringe to finish the pillows.

The Bathrooms

Bathrooms are for relaxing mind and body, but they must also be efficient. If the bathroom is yours alone, or shared with one other, you can concentrate more on the aesthetics. If this is a family bathroom, function may take precedence. Because the space is small, using expensive tiles, flooring and window treatments may not be beyond the budget. If you're lucky enough to have a modern bathroom that functions well, you can have a lot of fun imprinting it with your personal touch. While I tend to promote white for every room in the house, the bathroom is the one place you can go wild with color, texture and patterns.

If your bathroom is horribly cramped and outdated and in need of remodeling, you might be able to do a lot of it yourself, but you should hire a professional for rewiring and replumbing. Take the time to look through manufacturers' catalogs (available in home centers) for the types of fixtures, bath tubs and shower units, and floor coverings that might appeal to you. Home centers such as Home Depot and Builders Square have in-house professional designers who can advise you or even create the design right down to the shower curtain. Take advantage of these services for good ideas and working plans. You might not know all your options from just browsing through books and magazines. There are many bathroom showrooms in most major cities. Check to see if there's one in your area. An added plus is that you can save a great deal of money by getting everything you need at a discount home center.

If you can't remodel, consider changing the sink and

online help

www.homecenterweb.com
Building supplies for bathrooms, kitchens, closets, decks, landscaping and every other area of a house.

166

shower fixtures. This involves a plumber, but if you find fixtures that can be installed into the existing openings, it might not be a costly job. This is a good way to bring an old bathroom into the twenty-first century. It's not difficult to give an old bathroom a facelift.

At the very least a fresh coat of semigloss or glossy paint will do wonders to make an old bathroom look better. Consider painting the ceiling a pale peach or sky blue. Paint the trim around doors and the baseboard a contrasting color. For example, if the walls are ivory use a moss green for the trim and pale celery green on the ceiling.

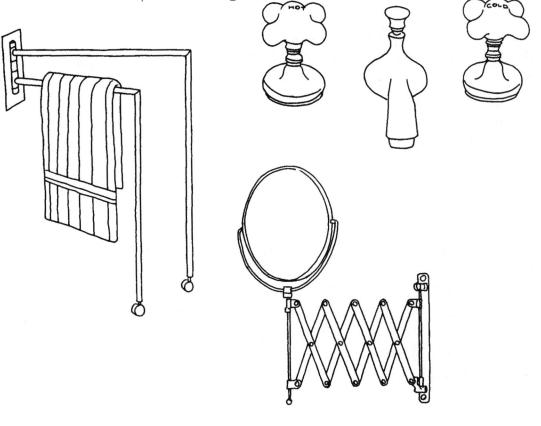

Space-Stretching Techniques

Most of us complain that we don't have enough space in the bathroom. The first thing you want to do is make the room seem streamlined. This means simple decorating.

1. Walls: White paint makes any room look larger and brighter. Mirror tiles on one wall are practical and room enlarging.

2. Windows: Fabric shades, such as the Duettes from Hunter Douglas, or miniblinds will give the window a sleek look. Wood shutters or louvered shutters achieve the same effect and offer flexibility for adjusting light and air circulation.

3. Find an area above the toilet or above the window where you can hang a deep shelf to hold towels.

4. Use a small wire cart with shelves (available in home centers) for holding bathroom essentials.

5. Roll towels into a basket and place it under the sink. Use a basket on the tub ledge to hold shampoo and body lotions. Or hang flat-back letter baskets or bicycle baskets on the wall to hold things.

Designer Victoria Hagan likes white, especially white terry.

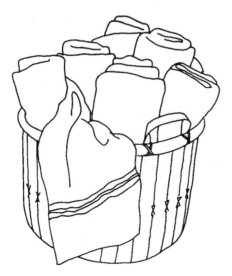

6. A narrow ledge around the tub area can be used to hold bath supplies as well as small plants.

7. Mount a swing-arm lamp on each side of the sink if you need more lighting.

8. Use the back of the toilet to hold a basket filled with pretty soaps. If you add a shelf over the toilet be sure there is ample room to remove the water tank if necessary.

9. If there's room for a small piece of furniture, such as a little bureau, end table or plant stand, such an item adds character and convenience.

10. I use wooden dowels that I stained and mounted with brass holders along two wall expanses for hanging towels.

11. Look for interesting shelving units or cabinets at yard sales for hanging in small wall areas. They can add storage and look good.

12. Add a strip of Shaker pegs (they come unfinished in different lengths at home centers) along a wall for hanging bathrobes and towels. Large brass or porcelain hooks mounted to the wall will do the same. Look for space on a narrow wall that might be found between the shower and door frame, for example. Hang a large hook to hold a bathrobe or towel.

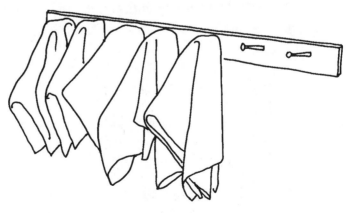

13. I installed a shelf between two walls above the baseboard next to the toilet. There was just enough space to accommodate an 8-inch-deep board, and it holds a basket of magazines and several ceramic containers of hand cream, shampoo and other toiletries.

14. A friend of mine uses a scrubbed pine armoire for holding towels and bathroom essentials. She doesn't have a medicine cabinet or any other storage unit, but the armoire, which is tall but shallow in depth, fits between the tub and the wall and holds it all. If you don't have room for a large piece of furniture, narrow bookshelves might do the trick.

15. Freestanding towel holders or quilt racks are excellent for holding different-size towels and washcloths in a bathroom where there is limited wall space for hanging adequate towel racks.

16. A small washstand is perfect for holding towels on the shelf below, as well as containers for makeup, brushes and a free-standing magnifying mirror. If possible, mount a towel bar or ring on one side.

17. It's easy to be creative with containers. I use a silver baby cup to hold cotton swabs, a votive candle holder for makeup brushes, a pretty sugar bowl for odds and ends, a small basket for brush and comb, and a ceramic crock to hold the hair dryer. Look around for unusual vases, terra-cotta planters or mugs that can be used to organize and assemble bathroom essentials right where you need them.

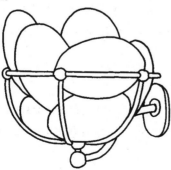

New Ideas for Old Bathrooms

Bathrooms can be wonderful little environments, created with just a few elements. You can do wonders with paint, wallpaper, fabric, floor covering and accessories. The bathroom is the one space you can transform with a little ingenuity.

A couple of years ago my husband and I took a plain, uninteresting powder room in a condominium and transformed it for a decorating magazine. The toilet and sink were plain white porcelain and the floor was covered with gray linoleum. The walls were painted light gray, and there was a large and obvious crack in the wall facing the door. The first thing we did was repair the crack with a putty knife and spackle. This takes minutes. Once the spackle dries, you simply sand it smooth.

Faux Finish for Walls

We then chose a light coral, semigloss latex paint to give the room a soft glow. Semigloss or glossy paint is better than flat latex paint for bathrooms because it is more durable and scrubbable. Once the first coat of paint was dry, we mixed the same color paint with a medium-tone glaze. Premixed transparent glazes come in light, medium and dark shades and are available in home centers. Mixing the glaze with paint in just the right proportions is easy to do by following the directions on the can. Using a natural sponge and the glaze mixture, we sponge-painted the walls to give them an overall texture. By mixing the glaze with the same color as the background, the sponging effect is very subtle and the walls become translucent, which gives them depth.

For the Finale

Self-sticking vinyl tile squares in a coral color were easy to install right over the linoleum floor. We painted a

Tip
For inexpensive luxury always use thick white towels and lots of scented candles.

narrow shelving unit, found in a thrift shop, deep green. This was placed against the wall between the toilet and sink to hold small plants, collectibles, folded guest towels and a ceramic dish filled with soaps. The finishing touch was a colorful painting by the homeowner that we hung on the wall where the crack used to be, just over the shelving unit.

An old-fashioned, ornately framed oval mirror (found in a seconds shop) fit on the wall over the sink, flanked by inexpensive, half-round wall lighting fixtures. We put a large, handcrafted clay pot with a flowering plant on the floor in a dead corner between the sink pedestal and the wall and filled a basket with multicolored hand towels to place on the back of the toilet. A wicker wastebasket was all that was needed to complete the simple but tastefully decorated room, which cost very little to make over.

Walls

Paint, vinyl wall coverings and ceramic or mirrored tiles are some of the options for redoing the walls. If you have wallpaper on the walls already and want to change the look, you can sometimes paint right over it if the paper isn't peeling or buckling and has been on for a long time. To rewallpaper you should first remove the old paper. There are liquid wallpaper solvents on the market that will remove the paper and hardened glue. If the wallpaper won't come off any other way, you may have to rent a steam machine specifically for this purpose.

"Shades of white give a room a beautifully balanced serenity," says designer Vicente Wolf.

The Power of Paint

Paint is the quickest, cheapest and easiest technique. Consider painting the entire room, including the ceiling, the same color. Or paint the trim in a contrasting color. If you choose a color for the walls, use bright white for the wood trim and ceiling. If the walls are tiled and unattractive, you can paint over them with epoxy paint. Always use semigloss or glossy paint in the bathroom because it's durable and scrubbable. Some professionals suggest oil-base paint. However, I always use latex because it's easy to clean up with water and the smell is not as strong or noxious. Paint in a well-ventilated space and wear a paint mask.

Wallpaper

Vinyl wallpaper is the most practical for the bathroom. You want to be sure it's moisture and mildew resistant as well as washable. Don't think because the room is small your choices of patterns are limited to small overall designs, or even light and airy ones. My favorite bathroom was the powder room in my very first house. It was a tiny, windowless room with a ventilating fan. I turned it into an elegant cocoon by laying down deep green, wall-to-wall carpeting (a sample piece was plenty) and wallpapering the walls and ceiling with a large cabbage rose print that also had large green leaves. It was sensational. I added rose-colored towels and accessories. When I had guests it was hard to drag them out of the room. It doesn't take much to make a small room look and feel luxurious.

If, however, you have a small, cramped bathroom that you want to brighten up, you can do this easily with colors that are warm and bright, such as peach, light blue, aqua or pale yellow. White always makes the room look fresh and bright and contemporary.

Tiles

Tiling walls and floors is a job that you can do yourself, but I usually recommend calling in a professional. It's worth getting an estimate and then figuring out what it will cost in materials and time to do it yourself. You may find that, because professionals buy the materials wholesale, in the long run you won't save that much by doing it yourself.

Mirrored tiles are available in self-sticking squares, and you can apply them to an entire wall or a small area.

Windows

A simple treatment like shades, blinds, shutters or café curtains is more practical than a more elaborate one. Because I don't like a prescribed window treatment in either the master bathroom or the powder room, I soften the windows with a valance fabricated from linen napkins and a tension rod. No sewing, no installation. You can use any size napkin, plain or patterned. Lace-edged white or ecru napkins look best. Place one napkin on the diagonal over the center of the rod. Add another napkin on each side so it overlaps the center napkin slightly to create a zigzag effect. Continue to add two more napkins if needed. If I want to cover the bottom half of the window, I drape a pretty tea cloth on the diagonal over another tension rod set across the center of the windows. If you need privacy, install a plain roller blind inside the frame behind the valance.

A lace panel hung from the top of the frame to the sill is another simple way to soften a bathroom window, provide some privacy and allow light to filter through. Or hang a lace-edged valance and line the windowsill with flowering potted plants in pretty containers.

Wooden blinds, louvered shutters or fabric shades can all be topped with a soft fabric valance for a finishing touch. A roller shade can be installed at the bottom of the window and pulled up for privacy on the bottom half of the window (see illustration on page 44).

Finishing Touches

There are many ways to make any bathroom more attractive. The finishing touches include coordinated towels, plant holders, interesting perfume bottles, ceramic containers, towel racks, and shower curtains. For an all-white theme, I always use fluffy, oversized bath towels in neutral colors. A white gardenia plant in a white ceramic soup tureen or interesting bowl is lovely on a wicker plant stand, a whitewashed, old-fashioned washstand or a small footstool. The deep green leaves of the gardenia plant add just the right color accent, and when the flowers are in bloom, they give off a wonderful scent. These plants do well in a humid environment.

Shower and Window Curtains

Use decorative, inexpensive sheets to make a window curtain and matching shower curtain. This is one time when a cheap sheet is best. Polyester is better than 100 percent cotton because the sizing makes the material stiff and the fabric won't wrinkle in a moist environment. A sheet with a pretty border gives you the option of a curtain with a border at the top or bottom. If you want the finishing touch of matching towels, buy an extra single sheet, cut off the border and apply it to the edge of the towels. Another way to customize plain towels is to add a border of ribbon, eyelet or rickrack.

Many decorators like to add something antique to a modern bathroom, for a bit of posh.

Pretty Containers

Look for interesting containers to hold Q-Tips, makeup brushes, cotton balls, bath beads and shampoo. Rather than hiding these items in a medicine cabinet, keep them out and use them to arrange an interesting display.

I always pore over catalogs from such places as Pottery Barn and Crate & Barrel, more for ideas than for things to purchase. For example, I have a silver tea set in an art deco design that I inherited from my grandmother. I never use it because I rarely serve tea, but I often use it as a vase for a bit of elegance on the bathroom vanity. The creamer holds cotton makeup pads. It's easy to find inexpensive painted vases in interesting shapes to be used for holding everyday things. Group a few silver and glass containers on a silver tray. Yard sales and thrift shops are wonderful sources for all sorts of pretty containers. I especially like old terra-cotta plant pots to hold odds and ends.

Plants Do Well in Moist Rooms

There are many plants that thrive in the humid environment of a bathroom if there is enough natural light as well. Plants make wonderful decorating accessories. Even if the bathroom is old and uninteresting, plants will definitely distract the eye. A large potted rubber plant or hibiscus can sit on the floor if the room is large enough. Ferns and ivy also do well in a bathroom.

Lighting Tricks

Even if you have overhead lighting or chase lights around the mirror, consider a small table lamp, especially in the powder room. When you have guests, leave this light on rather than switching on the brighter lights. Even the tiniest space will hold a small bedroom lamp with a 40-watt bulb. A pink bulb creates a rosy effect and gives off a subtle glow.

Fashion designer Anna Sui loves a shower curtain when it becomes part of the room. She says, "It becomes like a fourth wall."

Martha Stewart hates shower curtains but says, "If you have one, it should be washable and you should wash it all the time."

Miniature Art Gallery

Photographs and artwork complete the picture. Treat a powder room that is used mostly for guests as if it's a miniature art gallery and fill the walls. I display framed photographs as well as drawings, framed cards and paintings from friends who are artists.

Displays in Small Spaces

Look for little niches to create a display. A corner shelf unit might work. In my bathroom I have an interesting carved shelf, salvaged from an old desk, over the toilet tank. It fits between the walls and holds an ever-changing display of nostalgic collectibles. There's a container of shells gathered on the beach, a flowerpot filled with miniature spools of colorful thread, a few framed photographs, a basket of ivory buttons and a ceramic dish that holds lavender and rosebud potpourri. Collectibles find their way into this area. The walls on each side of the vanity are filled with old family photographs. Even though the room is only 4 x 6 feet, I sometimes squeeze a small wicker plant stand into a corner to hold an array of miniature botanical picture books. Sometimes the plant stand is replaced with a stool that I painted and decorated with pressed flower petals. I try to make this room a surprise for my guests.

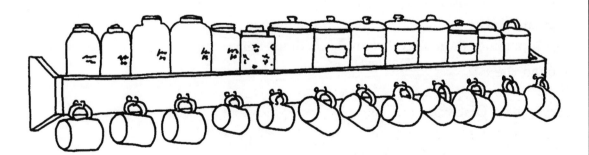

Rooms for Special Uses

There are over 40 million offices used by full- and part-time self-employed people. If you are among this growing group, or even if you only do the bookkeeping for your family, you need a place to work. If you can't spare an entire room, it's a good idea to create an out-of-the-way place to keep everything organized so you can work efficiently. Sewing and hobby rooms, workshops and laundry rooms are other spaces in your home that can be designed for personalized use.

Home Office

Setting up a home office, be it a room or a niche, requires an eye toward efficiency and comfort. The space can be as stylish as you want. Last year, our town's Decorator Showhouse fund-raising event included a home office. The house was built in the 1800s and, in keeping with the designs in the rest of the rooms, the office was decorated in an Early American style. A love seat was covered in practical but stylish fabric, the floor was painted and stenciled with an Amish quilt pattern as large as an area rug and antique boxes were converted into storage files. However, the room was also outfitted with all the electronic equipment needed and a streamlined desk with shelves for holding everything. It was smart, stylish and efficient.

Work Space

If your work space is a desk in the corner of the living room or a niche in the kitchen, be sure it is well lit,

Tip
Lighting affects the way we feel when we're in a room.

protected from children's curious fingers and not in the direct path of a busy passageway. If you don't have a bedroom available, consider creating an office space in a basement, garage or attic. An attic offers isolation from the rest of the house and can become a very private space. My office was created from minimal attic space above my husband's studio. We installed a circular stairway for access, a window at each end of the room and a skylight in the sloping roof. It did not require any major exterior building. We designed the room as a feature story for *Woman's Day* magazine in order to show how anyone could find room at the top for minimal cost.

Even a closet can be converted into a small work area for housing a desk, end to end, with built-in shelves

and files on either side. Look over every square inch of your home, room by room, and ask yourself, Where can I steal some space? Then ask yourself what work you'll do there, how much space would be ideal and how little space you can realistically live with.

Basic Plan

One of the best things about working at home is that there are no rules. When it comes to decorating, you can do it any way you please. You are in a position to make all the decisions. While you'll want it to function efficiently, you'll also want a space that is appealing and cozy so you'll enjoy being there. Decide what are the most important things for achieving this. For me they were wall-to-wall carpeting and an entire wall of storage. I also wanted the room to be light and bright, with a soft sofa or chair for relaxing between long hours at the computer.

Wall-to-wall carpeting on a home-office floor will help to soundproof the room and make it feel warmer.

Begin by making a list of everything you think your home office should have. Using graph paper, roughly draw all the stationary items in place. Next to each item that will take up floor space, write down its dimensions. You can get these measurements from office furniture catalogs.

When planning the layout of the room, position the desk where you will get the most natural light. I like to have stretching space and my desk is next to a window for occasional "drifting into space." You need to plan for storage of office materials, which might be on shelves, in a well-organized closet system or in a free-standing storage unit.

When planning surface space, itemize the equipment you'll be using. Most offices have a fax machine, computer, printer, answering machine and telephone. Be sure you have adequate electrical and telephone outlets. You'll also need a separate work surface to spread out papers for research and for occasional handwriting chores, such as check writing, notes and personal correspondence.

If you're stealing space from public rooms in the house, try to create a multipurpose environment so you can put the work out of sight when you need to. This might require clever uses of room screens or a curtain divider at one end of a room, or cabinets to house equipment that can be brought out or stowed away easily.

Furniture Options

A home office does not have to be furnished with office furniture, although a good swivel desk chair with adjustable height and back support and a proper computer desk are essential. Office supply and furniture catalogs are great sources for inspiration and for selecting the basic equipment you'll need. Storage is key. You need space to store business papers and materials. A rolling utility cart can be used to hold a fax machine and stacks of paper. At the end of the day you can roll it easily into a closet if you need to get it out of the way.

Files don't have to be the metal office type. Catalogs such as those from Hold Everything, Pottery Barn and Crate & Barrel regularly offer handsome items such as wicker baskets, wooden boxes and other containers made to be used as file holders.

Storage

Assemble a storage wall with stock modular units that include cabinets, file drawers and pull-out shelves with a custom-made look. These items, with easy-to-care-for laminate finishes, are available in catalogs, discount stores, home centers and office furniture outlets.

Bookshelves take up little space but hold lots of office necessities. Look for an interesting wall cabinet to add charm to the room as well as hidden storage. In my remodeled attic, the eaves on each side of the room slope down to less than four feet, which is too low to be usable. To make the most of this space, I bought inexpensive, unfinished wooden stock kitchen cabinets to place side by side on the floor along each wall. These cabinets are not very deep and they're made to fit right up to the ceiling in a kitchen, and so they don't have a finished top surface. I had a strip of pine board cut to the length of each wall and slightly deeper than the cabinets. When placed on top, it unifies the cabinets and the whole thing looks like a built-in unit. The cabinets provide two walls of storage for extra office supplies, and I have a surface shelf that spans two entire walls, without taking away any real room space.

Kinds of Cabinets

1. Stock cabinets are made in standard sizes so you can select the size to fit your needs. These are the least expensive. If they don't fit exactly in your space and there are only a few inches to fill at each side, you can do this with a space filler or facing board to give them a custom look.

2. If standard cabinets do not fit in your space, you can find semi-custom cabinets. These are standard units made in 3-inch increments. This gives you some flexibility to better accommodate your space.

3. Custom cabinets are the most expensive and are made to your exact measurements.

4. Cabinets come in a wide variety of sizes, styles and finishes and can be used for almost any storage situation, from built-in wall-to-wall cabinetry to hanging a single cabinet on an office wall.

Lighting

Good lighting is important. For me, this translates into a lamp on every surface. Two windows and a skylight provide plenty of natural light in my office by day. However, I often work late and I want plenty of light. Make the most of natural light from windows for general lighting. Light-controlling blinds are good-looking and practical, and you'll be able to control glare. But you'll also need task lighting. A desk lamp with a halogen bulb is bright as well as easy on the eyes. You can use any swing-arm-type lamp, but even a clamp-on desk lamp can be adjusted to throw light where you want it. I also like a good-looking table lamp for ambience in the room. While my desk area is brightly lit, this lamp bathes the rest of the room in soft lighting and makes it more inviting at the end of the day.

Decorative Touches

Now that you've figured out where to put all the office equipment, it's time to decorate. A rug on the floor; a small sofa if there's room; pictures on the wall; small, homey artifacts on the shelves; flowers and plants; maybe a quilted wall hanging—these are some of the things that might go into personalizing the space.

I have a daybed in my office for the occasional overnight guest. It's narrow and has a wood frame stained to match the cabinets. The mattress is covered with a fitted patchwork quilt and there are large pillows against the wall for comfortable sitting. The pillows are covered in fabrics to match the quilt and it looks more like a sofa than a bed. This is where visitors sit, or where I take a break from my work. A 24-inch-square patchwork wall hanging and a framed poster fill the stairway wall. I have several framed salvaged pieces of old patchwork quilts. There are photographs of my family on the storage shelf, and even though the room is completely carpeted I use a small hooked rug in front of the daybed for accent and color.

Don't be bound by conventional office decor. Consider using the decorative touches that would enhance any other room. Fresh flowers, potted plants, a ficus tree, a piece of sculpture, art, framed photographs and collectibles are just a few ideas. If your office doubles as a guest room, make it as comfortable and warm as possible without giving up any convenience.

Family Distractions

A friend of mine has a home office that's mostly off-limits to her family. However, she stocks a special shelf for her children. This shelf holds baskets with their "office supplies" and she keeps it replenished with cray-

Tip
Table lamps enhance and complement the look of a room. They shouldn't be an afterthought.

ons, colored pencils, lots of paper, stickers, a stapler, erasers, and rulers. They are not allowed to take these items out of the office, but she has special times when they can work with her.

Instant Office

If you have one wall you can devote to work space, you can create an efficient desk for your work. All you need is two filing cabinets (they can be secondhand) of the same height (but not necessarily the same style), a 30-inch-wide hollow-core door, satin-finish polyurethane, a 4-inch sponge brush and a can of spray paint.

1. Remove the drawers from the cabinets. If the files are rusty, sand them lightly.

2. Using a back-and-forth motion, spray paint the entire surface of each file. Repeat on the drawer fronts.

3. Coat the door with polyurethane. Let dry and recoat.

4. Place the door on top of the file supports at each end. This surface is deep enough to hold your computer, printer, paper holder and a bunch of containers for disks, pencils, telephone and lamp, with room left over for spreading papers out.

5. Since this desk is out in plain sight, the trick to making it look good is the accessories you use. A great desk lamp is essential. I like the green-shaded brass banker's lamps available through mail-order catalogs. Add a few framed photographs, a pretty vase to hold fresh flowers, a small clock and an interesting basket to hold clutter, especially when you aren't working. And never stick a freebie calendar on the wall with a push pin, no matter how tempting it is to do so. Framed paintings, posters or botanical prints will look infinitely better.

Resource:
Home Lighting Handbook
by General Electric,
800-626-2000

Laundry Rooms

Since most washers and dryers are in a basement, you'll probably have the space to create a laundry area. There's plenty you can do to make it most efficient with very little effort. Convenience is more important than looks. Some ideas include a continuous surface for folding laundry, open shelves to hold laundry baskets, rods for hanging permanent press items and baskets for holding bottles of bleach, spot remover and softener. Even if the space is limited, you might be able to fit a small, freestanding bookcase next to one of the appliances to hold detergents. Inexpensive laminate or unfinished furniture pieces are easily adapted for use in a laundry room.

A length of pine or plywood, even a narrow hollow-core door, can be supported on either end with saw horses or modular cubes for storage. Colorful plastic crates when stacked side by side and on top of one another make sturdy and useful supports as well. Install shelves above the wood surface and you'll have all the space you need.

Your basement walls will be more cheerful if you paint them a bright color or apply a sponge-painting technique to create a user-friendly area. Use a roller to apply a coat of flat white latex paint. Then sponge over the area with light blue, for example, using a natural sponge for a cloudlike effect.

Hobby Areas

Depending on your hobby, there's always some place to create an area that doesn't impinge on the rest of the house. Most people end up working on the dining or kitchen table, which means they have to schedule work between meals. It gets inconvenient at best and takes the spontaneity out of the creative process. Here's how one couple made a hobby area.

She makes quilts and he weaves baskets. They needed separate areas to keep their materials in an efficient way so they can work when they have spare time. To do this they each claimed a closet in their family room; his is a double closet, hers a single. He cut boards for desks to fit exactly the width and depth of each closet, end to end, and installed each of them at the appropriate work height in each closet. He likes to sit on a high stool, so his desk is at counter height. Her desk was positioned at the level most comfortable for sewing.

In her closet, he installed a Peg-Board on the back wall and narrow shelves from the desk to just below the ceiling on one side. On the other wall, he installed a swing-arm lamp. The sewing machine sits on the desktop. Packages of pins, spools of thread, scissors and measuring tapes hang or fit into baskets and containers that hang efficiently on the Peg-Board. Folded fabrics fit on the side shelves as well as in the bottom of the entertainment armoire in the family room. She has a fold-down ironing board attached to the inside of the closet door. They had an electrical outlet installed inside the closet for the sewing machine and iron. An office swivel chair completes her hobby area.

He attached a Peg-Board on the back wall of his closet as well, but installed a shelf, end to end, at the top of the closet to hold the baskets in progress. All basket-making materials are accommodated on the Peg-Board. A small cabinet under one side of the desk holds more materials.

When she is quilting, she uses a frame that's set up under a window for optimum natural light, and she uses the dining room table when she needs a large area for measuring and cutting fabric. When they're done for the day, they simply shut their closet doors and the work disappears.

If you can't devote a closet to crafting, consider setting it up as suggested for an instant home office.

Great Space-Saving Items

A trip to a good home center will reveal all sorts of handy items to organize office, hobby and workshop materials. You'll find racks, rolling carts, shelving, baskets and flexible storage systems.

1. A tool box to hold sewing accessories is easy to cart from one area to another and everything is held neatly.

2. Wire rolling carts can be outfitted with different size baskets to hold tools, fabrics, rolls of wrapping paper, laundry, picnic supplies or beach toys.

3. Rubbermaid plastic boxes can hold all sorts of odds and ends and keep things neatly stored on shelves in the garage, hobby room, attic or home office.

4. Large plastic recycling containers are perfect for keeping a garage shipshape. They're also good for holding large toys such as trucks and cars.

5. Lee/Rowan's ten-runner basket system can be used to form the base of a hobby/work table or a planter's potting bench in the garage or painter's area, or for holding sewing equipment, with the top used for cutting and pinning fabric.

6. Tilt baskets go on the wall or side by side on shelves. They are approximately 9 x 11 inches. You can see what's in them at a quick glance because the front is lower than the back.

7. Steel-rod industrial shelf units such as those used in commerical kitchens can be used to hold everything from media equipment to tools in the garage. The extra-deep shelves can be positioned at any height. These sturdy units made of chrome or enamel can support heavy objects and the open wire shelves won't collect dust.

8. Mobile garment racks are efficient closets that allow you to store extra clothes wherever you can find an out-of-the-way spot. They offer a solution for temporary clothes storage in a guest room or for storing winter coats in summer without using valuable closet space.

9. Wicker mail baskets are available in sizes to hold letters or magazines and can be mounted on a home office wall over the desk. This is a good way to organize daily mail clutter.

10. Rolling file cabinets shuttle your office from one room to another, but best of all you can slide the entire unit into a closet and out of the way when desired. Some are well designed in a variety of wood finishes so you aren't limited to the old-fashioned steel items.

11. Desktop items such as a magazine butler, business card holder, letter file basket, in-out tray and mail sorting basket keep everything neat and organized on your desk or on shelves. Put these items to use wherever you organize an area for paying bills and you'll be more efficient.

12. Wooden cubbies with wicker drawers are proportioned for holding office supplies or filing computer disks. Use them to create a custom arrangement.

Small Spaces

Every bit of space counts in your first home. Don't think that small spaces can't be interesting spaces. In fact, these are the most challenging and therefore the most interesting. Hallways, entryways, stairways and landings are special places for creating ambience and set the stage for the rooms leading from them. A real estate agent once described a house as having two and a half bedrooms. The half bedroom turned out to be nothing more than a closet, but when the new owner took over, she turned that little space into a sitting area that was more luxurious than any room in the house.

Decorating a small space in an exciting way is all about editing. If you're starting with nothing, you're in luck. You don't have to figure out what to get rid of. If you want the space to seem larger, don't fill it so it becomes claustrophobic. However, if a cozy, intimate look appeals to you, this is a lot easier to achieve than decorating on a grand scale. It all depends on how the space will be used.

Color

Very pale pastels are often better than white. White can actually look dull in low lighting. To make a small room look larger, paint the walls, ceiling and trim one color. The more contrast between the walls and the trim, the smaller the room will look. It will have a choppy feeling. This also goes for floors. Small area rugs aren't as space enhancing as a floor treatment of all one material and color. High-gloss paint will brighten a small space.

When asked what makes a room passé, designer Barbara Barry said, "Theme rooms."

Another designer says, "Nothing is passé if you really love it."

What's Hot

Wood venetian blinds

Large-scale furniture

Real comfort

Fresh flowers, one kind only

Mixing old with new

Sisal rugs

Simple, clean, uncluttered rooms

One really good piece of furniture

What's Not

Rooms that look like pictures of rooms

Clutter

Too much of any one thing

Matched sets

A decorator's package

Overtreated windows

Ruffled curtains

Too many fabrics, colors and textures

Portraits of somebody else's ancestors

Perfection

The late, great decorator Billy Baldwin lived in a small and undistinguished apartment in New York City. To overcome its size and plainness, the decorator painted every room dark brown, which was his trademark. He used off-white shades and brass accessories for accents and created illusions of space by placing mirrors in useless corners. Rather than concentrating on making the small rooms look larger, he made them look stylish and as good as he would have any other size room.

Focal Points

Most decorators agree that the success of a tiny space is having a focal point. This might be a wonderful piece of furniture, a painting or an unusual floor or wall treatment. You might paint the walls of a stairway in a bold color, or stencil the runners between stair treads. Black and white vinyl tiles set on the diagonal to form a diamond checkerboard pattern can make an entry or hallway quite dramatic. At the same time this is a good way to make a narrow hall seem wider and bigger. An attractive canvas floorcloth will become the focal point on a stair landing or in the entryway. Treat a hallway like a small room and use it as a gallery. Line the walls with framed family photographs.

If your room has a fireplace, this is a wonderful focal point around which to arrange furniture. Use the wall space above to hang one large picture or make a grouping. Fill the mantel with lots of interesting candle holders of different shapes and sizes. In summer, when the fireplace isn't used, fill it with an arrangement of dried flowers and grasses in a large basket.

An unusual chair or piece of folk art such as a weather vane or sculpture on a pedestal becomes the focal point in an entryway. It's easy to create a pretty and practical environment in a small entry with an interesting arrangement on a small table. All you need is a low table lamp, a pretty container for mail, a vase of flowers and perhaps a few framed pictures. Add a mirror on the wall above the table and you've created a warm and welcoming focal point in the room.

Lighting

Wall-mounted sconces and floor uplights provide indirect general lighting that is most effective in small areas. An uplight is a canister light about 8 inches high that can sit on the floor or a table. Here are some old tricks that decorators use to create indirect and dramatic lighting in an entryway: Place an uplight behind a large plant on the floor in a corner. A large chandelier centered on the ceiling in a small space gives it a magical quality. Light reflecting off the ceiling opens up a small room. An interesting lamp, perhaps an antique, with a translucent shade on a small table in a hallway will make the room look gracious.

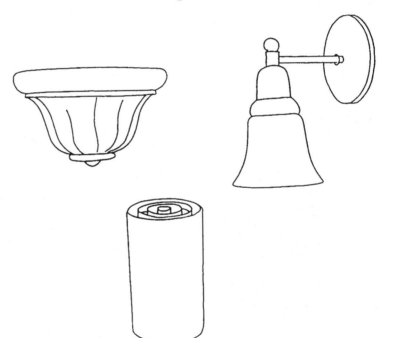

Walls

Strangely, small spaces seem larger when the walls are papered in a bold pattern. If you love pattern and color, use it in your hall or entryway for a great dramatic effect. This is a marvelous way to enhance a room that has nothing special in the way of architectural details. The wallpaper gives the room an assertive attitude. If, on the other hand, you have a period house, choose wallpaper of that style to give it back its heritage.

Windows

If the small space has a window, keep it bare so you can get as much natural light as possible. If you must treat it, keep it simple. Linen Roman shades from Pottery Barn are quite handsome. To make a small window appear larger, place a curtain rod as high as possible above the window frame and hang diaphanous, filmy curtains that puddle to the floor. The window will appear grander than it is and the curtains won't block the light.

Furniture

Any furniture you introduce into a small space should be oversized. This might seem like a contradiction, but small pieces will look dinky and make the room appear insignificant. A few bold pieces will dramatize the space.

Extras

Get high decorating impact from low-cost extras. For example, a large mirror will reflect light and expand the space. A large painting has more impact than a grouping of small ones. If you can't afford a painting, frame an interesting poster, calendar pages, photographs or greeting cards. Tip: Be sure to ask your framer for ultraviolet glass so the print won't fade when exposed to sunlight for an extended period of time. Tall plants or floor trees are more dramatic than small potted plants. However, a shelf filled with flowering plants in interesting containers will brighten the area and your spirits in the winter.

Decorator Mark Hampton says, "Patterned wallpaper makes a marvelous background for pictures. Hang different drawings and prints, combined with paintings, on an all over patterned background."

If you have an interesting collection of small objects, group them together to create an attractive tabletop display in an entryway. Set off the collection with one tall object, such as a lamp or a vase of flowers in just one color, so it doesn't overshadow the collection.

Run narrow ledge shelves equally spaced on one long wall above the sofa, for example, and create a wall of artwork in similar style frames. Break up the space with interesting objects such as a carved bird, a banded bowl or a pretty vase. Grouping the collection on one wall makes a more dynamic statement than if the objects and art were spread sparsely around the room. If you lean some of the art and photographs against the wall, or on a mantel, rather than hanging it all, you'll have the flexibility to rearrange at will and the arrangement is more interesting.

Accessories

When you walk into a beautiful room or see one that appeals to you in a magazine or book, you might not be able to identify exactly what makes it so wonderful. You only know you love it. This is usually because the room has personality. It may have gorgeous furniture, and the fabrics and colors may be exquisite, but it's the accessories that pull it all together. This is where individual style enters the picture. Pillows, vases of fresh flowers, paintings, framed photographs and posters, collectibles and books are the accessories that give a home personality and make it look lived in. Aside from the pictures on the walls, these are the things we move around until we find a pleasing arrangement. And even then we go on rearranging from time to time because this is what keeps our homes from becoming static. Most decorators will tell you that their own homes are always in flux. They are never finished. I like to refer to my home as a rough sketch. This is what creating a nest is all about. Decorating is the process of refinement and you have only yourself to please.

Aside from looking good, a room should feel good. The other day I was sitting in a friend's living room and realized that I was uncomfortable. There were too many things on all the surfaces. At other times I've been struck by the absence of things, making a room feel unlived in. It's important to strike a good balance with the right amount of accessories. This can be achieved by adding a little at a time and then taking away just one thing. You'll get a feel for what the room needs in this way. It's easy to add and subtract.

Collectibles

If you don't already have a passion for collecting and
haven't amassed a dozen blue Spode plates, for example,
almost anything you are attracted to can become the
basis for a group of related objects to match your decorating sensibilities. There is only one rule about collecting: Always buy what appeals to you, even if it has
no monetary value and isn't considered fashionable. For
example, a while ago, Early American patchwork quilts
were in great demand. They are still great folk art collectibles that give a home warmth and character, but
there are very good reproductions now and it's not so
difficult to find appealing designs within anyone's budget. The reproductions provide the decorating look if
you aren't collecting them for their historic or monetary
value.

Collecting is highly subjective. There are no hard-
and-fast rules. Keep in mind that a collection doesn't
have to be costly, and if it has sentimental value, it is
all the more interesting because it has a known history.
For example, the father of a young son built a narrow
shelf on the walls around his bedroom to hold a collection of tiny matchbook cars.

Some people collect things they can use, such as old
baskets. Nantucket lightship baskets are prized for
their exceptional craftsmanship, as well as the history
these baskets represent. They were made during long
watches at sea by Nantucket lightship keepers. These
baskets, old and new and of varying sizes and shapes,
are used to hold everything, and it isn't uncommon to

find several hanging from kitchen rafters in exquisitely preserved island homes. Shaker baskets from Maine and Indian baskets from the Southwest lend a different kind of variety to a collection. When used, their value is expanded beyond visual attractiveness.

I have seen many collections in the houses I've visited and photographed for my books, as well as those belonging to my well-traveled friends. They range from a delightful collection of English souvenir tins, metal toys and duck decoys to banded blue-and-white mixing bowls, wind-up alarm clocks, '50s lunch boxes and ceramic bunnies.

Inexpensive Accessorizing

Decorating with a collection can be greatly satisfying and, if you want to add style to a room for little money, a collection can fill the bill. There are so many interesting items to collect for display, giving a room instant character. For example, collecting old dishes of a particular period, design, color or style can be a lot of fun and can lead to a most enjoyable education. By collecting slowly, you have the opportunity to put together an interesting and varied group of items without spending a great deal all at once. On the other hand, if what you want is a pretty arrangement that makes a room look lived in, you can easily find a group of like items with which to create the semblance of a collection. Whether your collection is old or new, or a little of each, it will add to the interest in your home.

What Should I Collect?

If you're unsure about what might make an interesting collection for your home, consider the following: If you don't have a lot of space, think about small items that are easy to display, that is, if you don't mind all that dusting! Possibilities are small boxes, figurines, perfume

Richard Holley, a Houston, Texas, decorator, says, "Big accessories give rooms a feeling of grandeur."

Decorator Mark Hampton has this advice for people setting up their first home: "It's a good idea to look for pictures, prints, works on paper, things that give a room character. I love folk art, and frankly, one reason it's so appealing is that you can afford it."

bottles, ivory eyeglass cases, scrimshaw, paperweights and souvenir items. If you have a wall that can be used for display, consider plates or framed botanical prints. Lots of people collect teapots, and I've seen a lovely collection displayed on a sideboard in a dining room. On Nantucket Island, where I live, collecting marine objects is very popular. Perhaps there is something historic about the place where you live that would lend itself to a collection.

Color

One dominant color can be the basis for a collection. One of my friends has a house with a brick fireplace wall in the dining room. Above the mantel and filling most of the space on each side of the fireplace, she's hung her collection of beautiful blue-and-white plates. This color scheme is carried throughout the room in the fabrics used on the chair cushions and the curtains on the wall of windows opposite the fireplace.

Collections from Travels

Collecting often provides a focal point of travel and is a good way to integrate the things you find on vacation into your decorating scheme. My friend Gretchen collects Quimper, the French pottery of the Provence region. She travels often to France, where she is always on the lookout for a little piece to add to her collection, displayed in an interesting glass cabinet in her dining room. The cabinet itself is old and once belonged to a relative.

While traveling in Italy she bought regional pottery, and when she and her husband built their first home, she had a shelf incorporated around a sun room especially for displaying the various dishes. Whenever possible, she adds to this collection as well.

Collections with Value

Some people like to collect things that, over time, will increase in value. To decide what you might like to collect in this arena, it's best to do your homework. Take out books on various subjects of interest. Subscribe to antiques magazines and newspapers. You'll quickly find that it doesn't take long to learn a lot about a collectible. And once you're tuned in to something, you'll be amazed at how much more comes your way. Printed material, such as a magazine article or a news item in a newspaper or on television, will suddenly grab your attention where, in the past, it would have gone unnoticed.

Accidental Collection

Sometimes a collection happens by accident. Someone gives you a gift of a Venini glass vase, for example. While you may never have seen such an item or even heard of Venini, it's love at first sight. The vase is just what you needed to make the little end table you inherited from your grandmother look good in the living room.

You check the Internet for information about this Italian designer and find a world you never knew existed. You're hooked. You look for museums or galleries that show his work and when planning a vacation decide to go to Toronto, Canada, because you want to visit the Thebes Gallery. The owner is a specialist in twentieth-century Italian glass, notably, '20s and '40s Venini. This leads to other sources, and before you know it, you're planning future trips around galleries and antiques shops that carry your collectible.

Displaying Collections

Whether your collection is housed in a special case, displayed on a shelf or tabletop or spread throughout the house is entirely up to you. Many collectibles are best

Some things look great because you don't expect them to be there. They simply take you by surprise.

200

viewed in relation to one another. For example, my husband and I once photographed a marvelous collection of carved antique ivory canes for a style book. These canes were grouped together in an umbrella stand and displayed casually in the entryway of the house, as if they might be used. A group of the more interesting pieces were formally displayed in a specially designed cabinet nearby, lending drama and excitement to the collection. The individual pieces were quite lovely and seeing them in relation to one another made them all the more interesting.

Two talented men in my town own a store that features American folk art collectibles. Their personal collection of brightly colored glass vases and pitchers is displayed on a weathered farm bench on their stairway landing. Everything else in this area is white, which provides a most dramatic background for the collection and gives it an importance it might not otherwise command. How you display your treasures is an important aspect of decorating with them.

Designer Karin Blake says, "Design a room around one piece of fabulous folk art."

Books as Decoration

Many people incorporate books into their decor. A friend of mine has lived in and remodeled many houses, and the first thing she does is plan for a wall of bookcases in her living room. I have seen many houses designed by architect Hugh Newell Jacobson. Minimalism is his interior decorating trademark, but every house of his that I've seen has a living room wall of bookcases from floor to ceiling. Books make a room highly personal.

My collection of early illustrated children's books fills one long shelf in my bookcase. Other favorite books remind me of specific times when they enriched my life. When I look at my collection of botanical books, I remember the experience of buying each one in a different place. Antique bookstores stand out in my mind as highlights of my trips. I think of a little out-of-the-way musty cave of a bookstore in a small town along the Canal du Midi in France when I see the spine of a certain book on my shelf. The bookstores that line Charing Cross Road in London are immediately called up when I see my books on the wildflowers of Europe. And one book in particular reminds me of a great period of personal growth. Collections don't have to be of monetary value to be worthwhile. Collect what enriches your life in whatever way is meaningful to you.

Options for Decorating the Walls

There are many alternatives to expensive paintings for decorating walls. Framed posters present an interesting area of collecting with infinite possibilities. When my husband and I travel we buy illustrated postcards and greeting cards as well as souvenir posters. We often visit art galleries and have purchased posters of an artist's work we admire when we couldn't afford an

Comedian Richard Lewis says, "When I was growing up, my mother, who covered everything of value with plastic or doilies, never let me put anything up on the walls of my room. Little did she know that when I got this house—my first—I would go absolutely in the other direction. I decided to put everything I cherish on the walls—and every other surface—and not care."

original painting. When professionally matted and framed, they all have great decorating potential.

Quilts

A patchwork or appliqué quilt is a wonderful substitute for paintings. They can cover an entire wall, becoming the focal point in a room. Or hang a wall quilt in a hallway. A friend hung a crazy quilt on her stairway wall for visual effect and to absorb sound. Early geometric patterns are still being reproduced and revised today. They have a graphic quality that always looks contemporary. Two-color quilts, such as blue or red and white, are often used as room decorations and can look right at home with any style. I have a very old red-and-white quilt that I hang in my all-white living room during the holidays. A red poinsettia plant on the table beneath the quilt completes the picture.

Some people are reluctant to hang quilts on the wall, thinking they are too precious. Quite the reverse is true. Quilts were made to be used and even early antique quilts have been washed hundreds of times. New quilts are reasonably priced and often made of a cotton/poly blend. This makes them even more durable than an old quilt, and the more they're used, the better they will look.

A wall hanging needn't be a full-size quilt. There are many small quilt squares no larger than a quilt block that are perfect for small wall areas. The best thing about using quilted wall hangings is the variety of colors available. Almost any Early American quilt pattern can be made in solid or printed fabrics or a combination of both. Since most quilt patterns are based on geometric squares and triangles, this is an easy do-it-yourself project if you're on a tight budget.

Quilts warm up any area of a room, adding color, texture and a feeling of coziness. If you're lucky enough to

A room should be punctuated with interesting details.

have inherited a quilt or two, don't pack them away to yellow in a closet or drawer. Quilts add a touch of Americana to any room, and something from your family's past combined with the new adds character and substance to any decorating scheme.

Paintings and Frames

Original paintings don't have to break the budget. You may not be able to afford a major work of art, but you can find lesser-known artists whose work you like, and little by little you can begin to acquire their paintings for your home. If you love an artist's work, begin with small affordable paintings until you can afford a larger piece.

If you have several small paintings but none important enough to stand alone, group them together or hang a large mirror and surround it with the framed artwork.

How something is framed is as important as what is being framed. Some decorators suggest using a uniform system for everything that will hang on one wall regardless of subject. Others, such as Mark Hampton, use different frames for pictures that will hang together to avoid a mass-produced look. Since framing materials come in numerous styles, colors and textures, go to a professional framer who can provide you with a wide selection of moldings and mats and who can advise you on the appropriate treatment for your art.

Hats

In one of the most stylish homes we've ever photographed, the walls in the entryway were decorated with a variety of hats. There were straw summer hats sporting scarves or large artificial sunflowers, a child's horseback-riding hat, and a few baseball caps on large brass hooks that had been carefully spaced in an artful arrangement. Completing the grouping was a small oval

The decorators at Thomas Britt Inc. like to create drama by placing mirrors opposite one another for infinite reflections.

mirror in an ornate gold-leaf frame next to a brass wall sconce. Since these items were used by the inhabitants, the display was practical as well as charming.

Plants and Flowers

Warm up your rooms with healthy green plants. You get a lot of visual impact from a good-size indoor tree. Decorator Barbara Barry says, "Green is my neutral—from pond scum to apple, sage to chartreuse." Plants and white flowers with bright green leaves in white or clear glass vases are perfect accessories in green and white rooms. Use flowers as an accessory theme and carry it through with framed botanical prints or watercolors on the walls.

Many contemporary designers have a common attitude about the use of flowers in decorating. The current trend is to use fewer flowers in an arrangement and, whether the same or different species, they should all be the same color. Leaves should be stripped from stems of fresh-cut flowers.

There was a time, not so long ago, when it was chic to use gimmicky containers such as an old teapot or an Early American grain scoop for holding flowers and plants. The style is now just the opposite. In fact, the more straightforward the container and the arrangement, the better. A single beautiful flowering blossom in a heavy cut-glass vase is currently the decorative accessory of choice.

Small plants clustered together are considered passé. One large plant is better. There are all sorts of exotic plants to choose from, depending on where you live. It's interesting to cultivate an unusual plant as a decorative accessory.

When Washington, D.C., designer Mary Douglas Drysdale was interviewed in *Traditional Home* magazine she said, "I realize that most people don't want to start from scratch, nor should they. Part of traditionalism is carrying on the heritage of your family, integrating things you have and may not see the value of—giving these pieces new life in a new scheme."

Outdoor Living

Make your outdoor living space an extension of your living room, and just as appealing. If you have a deck, patio, porch or lawn area, it will double your living space. The operative words for outdoor decorating are casual, carefree and comfortable. If you invest in good-looking outdoor furniture, such as wicker, rattan or wrought iron, you'll find it can work indoors as well. This is especially useful if you live in an area where you don't have warm weather year round. It's also helpful if you can't buy all your furnishings for every room in the house right away—some pieces can do double duty for part of the year. I have wonderful, oversized deep-green wicker chairs reminiscent of the 1920s; they're good reproductions made by Lloyd Flanders. The cushions are covered with weather-resistant fabric, and I made throw pillows with chintz floral fabric to match the summer slipcovers in the living room. They provide comfort and look great on my deck all summer, and in winter, I use them in my sun room. I use smaller white wicker chairs around the outdoor wrought-iron dining table, and move them about for casual seating as well.

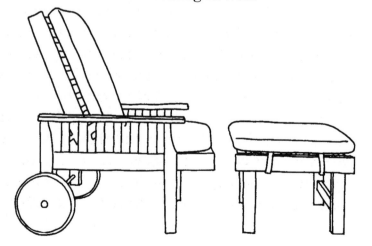

Furniture

There is as much variety in outdoor furniture today as you'll find in all other home furnishings. Wicker furniture is perfect for an enclosed porch or in an open area where the weather isn't too harsh. It has a relaxed, lazy summer-day feeling. Wrought-iron furniture is classic and will give you years of comfort and style. Aluminum is sturdy and will resist the effects of water and sun. It's most practical by the pool or for a beach house.

When shopping for outdoor furniture, decide first what you'll need for your outdoor activities, and consider the climate conditions. If you enjoy eating outdoors, you'll want a table and chairs. You may want an outdoor umbrella over your table, in which case, think about a round table with a hole in the center for this purpose. Market umbrellas are quite popular and handsome. While they used to come only in natural canvas, they are now available in colors as well as printed fabric. The poles are made of wood. The originals are quite expensive, but there are now copies that look every bit as good, but are quite affordable. I've seen them in two or three sizes in discount centers, catalogs and even my local supermarket. If you like to relax in the sun, you might want a chaise longue. An occasional table or two is handy and you may want a coffee table.

When planning the layout of your outdoor living space, you can be a lot more casual than in designing the layout for your living room. If the furniture is lightweight, it's easy to move it around for different situations—for example, optimum sunning at different times of the day. Or use chairs around a dining table and the same chairs arranged for casual conversation.

Color

If you're not sure how to make the most of your outdoor room, take a look through garden magazines. Use the flowers and their colors for inspiration. Blue and white have always been popular. Add little accent touches of yellow and this color scheme sings. Blue and white with accents of watermelon pink make another pretty outdoor color scheme.

You don't have to stick to one or two colors here. Use a riot of colors in a fabric print. For example, you might choose one solid color for your seat cushions and then add throw pillows made from a bright floral print. Even if frilly isn't your style of decorating indoors, you'll find that big, fluffy pillows with ruffles work here. Go overboard in the pretty department.

Hunter green and white are a classic color combination for outdoor living. Many furniture companies use this deep green color for their furniture. You'll find wrought-iron furniture in black and white as well. Ticking fabric is quite good-looking, and you can find it in a variety of colors such as green, red, pink, navy and black with white. This fabric is serviceable and sturdy even if it isn't coated for outdoor use. So long as the covers can be removed for easy washing you can't go wrong. Keep in mind that dark colors absorb heat, and light colors repel heat. Therefore, if you live in a hot climate, you may not want deep-green canvas seat cushions.

In certain areas of the country, like the South, the sun is much brighter, so we tend to use more intense colors. In the Northeast, the light is more diffused and even subtle colors appear to be much brighter. Pale shades look best.

On one occasion, while styling furniture around a pool for a magazine assignment in the South, we chose a vivid color scheme of aqua, turquoise, fuchsia and marine blue. We found inexpensive polyester sheets in those colors at a local Kmart. We then cut them into 25-inch squares, stitched them together and stuffed them with poly stuffing (sold in packages at all discount and sewing stores) to make a bunch of oversized pillow cushions. We tossed these around the pool and used them to soften the brightly colored Adirondack chairs we had painted in matching colors.

Fabric

There are many innovations in outdoor cushions. Some are covered with fabrics treated for weather resistance. They will dry quickly and are mildew-proof. This is essential if you live in an area with high humidity. Since I live on an island, this is extremely important. I spend a lot of time in Key West, Florida, as well, so I've had the advantage of outdoor living in the North as well as the South. Each comes with its special considerations in regard to outdoor furnishings. While my basic seat cushions are weather resistant, I love the look of chintz throw pillows on my wicker outdoor furniture. Since everything gets damp at night where I live, I keep a large basket by the French doors leading to the deck. Each night I simply gather up the pillows, tossing them into the basket until morning when I spread them about again. It's a minor inconvenience.

If you want to make your own cushions, look for pretty sheets to use for your covers. You get a lot of fabric for little money. They come in so many different colors and patterns, and the material is wonderfully cool to sit on and practical to take care of. Polyester actually resists moisture.

Fabric shops carry a broad selection of stain- and weather-resistant materials made for outdoor use. Canvas, for example, comes in all different colors and is often used to cover seat cushions on boats. Many companies, such as Lloyd Flanders and Brown Jordan, known for their fine outdoor furniture, have a range of cushions covered in weatherproof fabrics that look elegant and soft but have the advantage of being practical for outdoor use.

Accessories

Plants, plant stands, plant containers, lanterns and floor coverings add up to luxury. Outdoors, as with any room in the house, the accessories give the space your personal touch. A rattan or sisal rug is a practical floor covering on a deck. If you don't have a garden, create your own in large containers. This gives you the advantage of being able to move them wherever needed for color and liveliness as well as for optimum sun and shade.

Look for any unusual objects that can serve as plant containers or plant stands to give your outdoor room personality. A friend of mine hangs a birdcage filled with bright pink geraniums from the roof of her porch. Around her deck, another friend has lots of mismatched wicker plant stands found at secondhand shops. Topiary trees, hanging ferns, a bird bath on a pedestal, an old metal milk can filled with wildflowers, a hanging lantern, votive candles, a hammock loaded with colorful pillows and a pretty pitcher to hold flowers are some of the decorative items you might use. A decorator in Key West grows orchids and hangs them from the spokes of her market umbrella over the table.

Candles always make dining outdoors romantic. The more votives and hurricane lamps you have on tabletops the better. The same decorator in Key West uses lots of clear Christmas tree lights all year long for decorating the deck. She recommends winding them around the umbrella pole, stringing them along a fence, and wrapping strands around trees surrounding the deck and wherever else you need sparkle. As dusk falls, your outdoor living room will be lit with the tiny lights. Even when viewed from indoors, these lights look wonderful on the deck or patio.

Additional Help

Painting

Painting is one of the easiest do-it-yourself projects and the one job in home decorating and improvement that most people tackle. This is partially because of the minimal investment of tools and the skills aren't hard to pick up. If you haven't hired a professional and you're planning to paint yourself, here are a few tips for doing it like a pro.

1. Allocate enough time for preparation and cleanup. And two painters are better than one. One person can be using the roller while the other is using a brush for painting near baseboards and ceiling trim.

2. Quality paint gives better coverage than inexpensive paint. If you scrimp on paint, there's a good chance you'll have to repaint sooner than you'll want to. A good paint job should last six or seven years, less for the kitchen.

3. If the walls are old and cracked, they'll need a primer sealer and two coats of paint, especially if the paint is a light color. Badly cracked areas must first be patched with spackle, then sanded smooth.

4. To determine how much paint you need, calculate the square footage of the room, then subtract the doors and windows and any areas you won't paint. If you're going to paint the ceiling, you need this measurement as well. A gallon of paint covers approximately 350 square feet. Never buy a gallon and 3 quarts. Always round off to a full gallon since you can use the extra for touch-ups later on. Most rooms require a primer and two coats of paint.

> Painting is like cooking: If you assemble everything you need beforehand, the job will be easier. With just the right background music, the job becomes fun.

213

5. Latex paint has a water base and is easy to clean with water. Oil-based paint is thinned with mineral spirits, which are used to clean the brush and rollers. Both types of paint are available in matte, semigloss and glossy finishes. If this is your first painting project, I would recommend flat or semigloss latex paint. It goes on easily, cleans up with water, dries quickly and doesn't give off noxious fumes. Ventilating the room is necessary for all types of paint, but applying oil-based paint is particularly hazardous. You should wear a paint mask and work on a dry, sunny day. It will take two or three days for oil-based paint to dry. Latex paint dries in a couple of hours.

Semigloss or glossy latex is often used on baseboards and window and door trim.

Preparation

1. Before you begin, cover the floor with a drop cloth or sheet of plastic (available in the paint section of your home center). Tape it down with easy-to-remove painter's tape made for this purpose. The tape won't leave sticky residue on carpets, floors or walls.

2. Put all the furniture together in the center of the room so you have plenty of space to work in. Cover the furniture with plastic down to the floor.

3. Remove all switch plates and hardware that won't be painted and put them in separate plastic bags or envelopes marked with their locations.

4. Light the room well. You'll find inexpensive clamp-on metal reflector lights in home centers. Two or three are excellent for clamping to ladders, shelves or doors and can be moved as the work proceeds around the room.

The higher the sheen, the easier to clean.

Tools

If you have a work table this will make the project easier and save you from constantly bending to get things from the floor. Cover it with plastic. A sheet of plywood on two sawhorses is good. You'll need the following:

1. Utility knife and razor blades for scraping paint from windowpanes. No matter how carefully you paint the window trim, getting paint on the panes is almost inevitable, but it's easy to remove when dry.

2. Clean rags.

3. Natural bristle brushes for oil paint, nylon or sponge brushes for latex paint. You will need these to paint baseboards, window and door trim, and the top and bottom of the wall area that can't be painted with a roller. You will need 4-inch brushes for doors and top and bottom wall areas, 2-inch brushes for window trim and baseboards, and a narrow brush for window sashes.

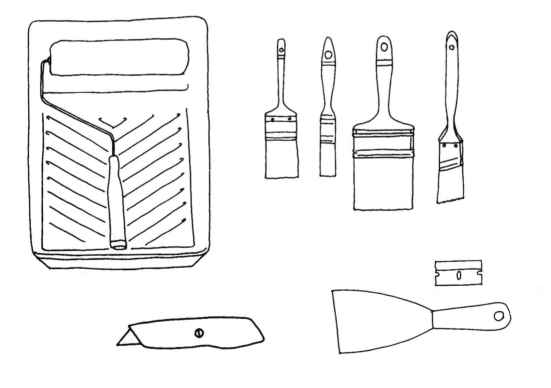

4. Roller and tray (buy a roller for each color paint).

5. Painter's gloves.

6. Plastic or cardboard paint buckets.

7. Coffee cans for soaking wet brushes.

8. Stirring sticks.

9. An extension pole to attach to the roller handle if you're painting the ceiling. Also good for high walls.

How to Do It

1. If the walls have any imperfections, you first must sand them smooth with a fine sandpaper, such as #200 grade. Clean up any sand dust with a damp rag or vacuum.

2. If there is any grease on the walls, they should be washed with warm water and detergent. If there is any mildew on the walls (black-green splotchy stains), add chlorine bleach or mildew disinfectant to the water. Some paint professionals recommend adding a mildew detracting agent to paint before applying it to walls,

How to Refinish Kitchen Cabinets

Use semigloss or glossy latex enamel to paint cabinets. It looks sharp and lasts longer than flat latex. It's also tougher and stain resistant, and has greater mildew resistance than oil-based paint.

Tools for Painting Cabinet Doors

• A good brush (it feels better and the job ends up looking better)

• Sandpaper in different grades

• Sealer and a sponge brush to apply it

• The best-quality paint you can afford

• Drop cloth and cleanup rags

• Screwdriver to remove hinges from doors

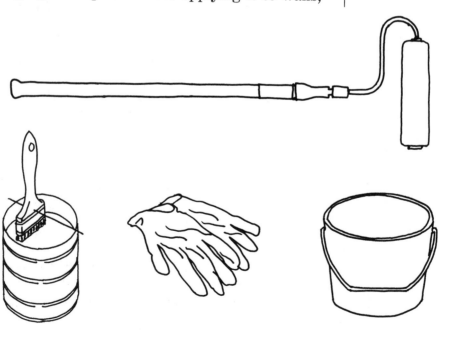

especially in the bathroom and kitchen. Ask your paint dealer about this when buying your paint. If there are residual cigarette smoke stains on walls or ceiling, apply a coat of paint.

3. Apply the first coat, which is your primer. Let dry according to directions on the can.

4. Professional painters usually open all the cans of paint, mix them thoroughly and pour them into one large bucket. Then they mix them all together and pour the paint back into the cans, so there is no variation in color from one can to the next. This is the way to do it right. However, if you don't do this, mix the opened can thoroughly. When I open a fresh can of paint, I use a ham-

Primer

A primer is a sealer that prepares the surface for painting. On bare wood it will cover knots and discolorations. On a previously painted surface it will cover repairs and spackling. Primer dries fast. Two coats will ensure a good result when the paint is applied.

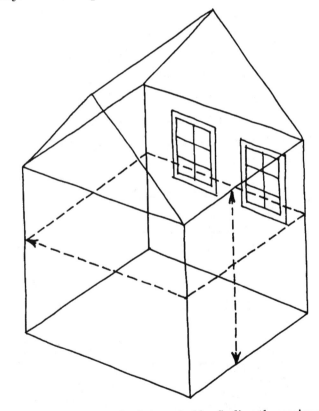

Determine the amount of paint needed by finding the perimeter of the room by adding the lengths of each wall together, then multiply this figure by the ceiling height. Subtract 20 square feet for each door and 15 square feet for each window.

mer and large nail to make a few evenly spaced holes around the inside of the rim where the lid was removed. In this way, when I draw the paintbrush from the can, the excess paint that usually collects in the ridge all around drips back into the can. When I put the top back on the can, it seals more firmly and keeps air from spoiling the paint.

5. Pour a small amount of paint into the roller tray.

6. Paint the ceiling first. Use the brush to paint from the edges out about 3 inches and continue rolling the paint on, blending the brushed-on areas while they're still wet.

7. When the ceiling is finished, do all the walls the same way. Always start with the wall opposite the doorway.

8. Paint all trim last, using the appropriate-size brush.

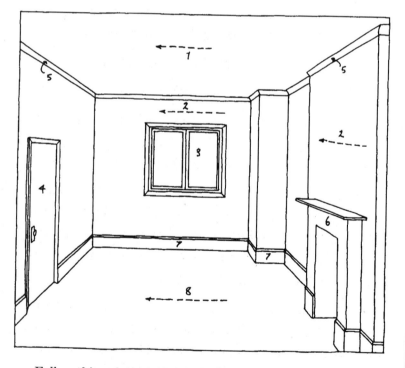

Follow this painting sequence: 1.ceiling 2.walls 3.windows 4.doors 5.moldings 6.fireplace 7.baseboards 8.floor

online help
National Decorating Products Association
www.hygexpo.com/ndpa/
Painting and wallpapering in a decorating context. This is an excellent place to get advice. Frequently asked questions are answered for you.

Special Techniques

Sponging, combing, rag rolling and stenciling are some of the faux finishing techniques that can be applied to walls with paint. These are inexpensive, relatively easy ways to add color and texture to walls, giving the room a focal point and adding interest to a room with no particular architectural details.

Sponging

This technique involves dabbing paint onto a solid painted surface to create a subtle pattern. You'll need a natural sponge, rubber gloves and paint (latex or oil-based) in a color contrasting with the wall color. You can add a glazing agent to the paint to give the wall depth and luster. The glaze can be mixed with the same color paint as the background to produce a very subtle texture. Or you can use white over light blue, or a slightly darker or lighter shade of the same color.

1. Spread newspaper over the work surface.

2. Dampen the sponge so it's soft. Squeeze dry.

3. Pour a little paint into a dish and dab the sponge into it. Then rub some of the paint off onto the newspaper and practice your pouncing technique on the paper.

4. Begin at the top of the wall and work on the space a patch at a time. Sponge over the wall quickly until the paint begins to fade. Reload the sponge, wipe away any excess so you don't get big splotches of paint on the wall, and continue to cover the area.

5. Stand back to assess your work from time to time. You can keep perfecting the look by going over it as many times as you think necessary. The trick is to have a subtle, overall texture that is almost cloudlike. Avoid obvious contrast.

Tip

For best results use two shades of the same color for a sponged effect. When you apply a dark color over a light background or a light color over a dark background the contrast is too harsh.

Combing

For this technique you'll need a tool that looks like a squeegee. The notched rubber strip enables you to drag a top coat of paint or glaze down the walls to produce a pattern of combed lines. You can create straight lines or curved lines, or even a checkerboard pattern. These tools are available in hobby and paint stores.

1. The base coat on your walls must be dry. Then a second, contrasting coat of paint or glaze is applied. The combing must be done while the paint is wet, so you might want to make this a two-person job. One paints, the other combs. Otherwise, you'll have to paint a strip, comb, then continue in this way.

2. Begin at the top corner of the wall and drag the comb over the wall with one long, smooth stroke. Wipe the paint off the combing tool after each swipe. When you start a new strip, overlap the first slightly. This is not an exact science. Irregularity in this type of faux finish is acceptable.

Rag Rolling

The effect of rag rolling is often compared to the pattern on moiré fabric. Some experts use rags, while others like plastic wrap. In either case, the process involves wadding up the material and using it to roll over a preglazed or painted wall while it is wet so as to produce a textured effect. If paint is used, it should be semigloss or glossy. You must complete an entire wall at one time for best results. It's even a good idea to do the whole room at once. Wear rubber gloves for this one.

1. Begin by preparing several rolls of wrap or rags so you can change them when they get too saturated.

2. Brush a wide strip of glaze over the wall. Starting at the top, roll through the glaze this way and that. As

Tip
Cheesecloth is a good material for rag rolling. It's available in hardware stores and home centers.

you continue down and across the wall, overlap so you don't have any sharp delineations and the entire wall is a continuous pattern.

Spattering

This technique can be used on anything from a small piece of furniture to an entire floor. It just depends on the size of the brush. A paint-loaded brush is knocked against a stick so that the paint flies off the brush in dots. For small projects a toothbrush is often used. On a floor use a large brush and sturdy stick.

You can test different effects such as white dots over a dark ground, dark over light, or multicolored dots. Whatever the combination, the result tends to be an overall texture of even consistency because the dots are fairly regular.

Wrap the stick with a rag to limit vibration, rap the loaded brush against the stick over a test area or rag to judge the size of the dots, and just continue until you get the effect you like.

This is a messy technique. Use gloves, eye protection and plenty of drop cloths to protect the surroundings.

Stenciling

A stencil is a die-cut pattern that's used to apply a design to a surface such as a wall. Using a special type of stiff bristle brush, you apply paint with an up and down pouncing motion over the cutout areas. When the stencil is removed, the painted design is revealed on the wall.

You'll find a wide variety of pre-cut stencil designs for creating borders, overall motifs resembling wallpaper, and murals in hobby and craft stores. Stenciled designs are used to add architectural interest and to highlight an area with hand painting. It's a good way to decorate any room. Choose the design and colors that best suit your decorating style.

1. Carefully plan the placement of your stencil designs. If you're stenciling a border around a room, measure the stencil and the area to which it will be applied so you can alter the design if necessary. For example, you don't want to end in the middle of a flower. Space the placement of each stencil element so you don't end awkwardly. Use a level and lightly mark the area in which the design will be contained so you keep it straight.

2. If the design requires more than one color, you'll want stencil all the areas in one color only all the way around the room before applying the next color.

3. Secure the stencil to the wall with masking tape.

4. The trick to a successful project is to keep your brush practically dry. Therefore, dip your brush lightly into the first color paint to be used. Pounce the brush up and down on newspaper a few times to remove excess paint.

5. Press one hand firmly against the stencil while applying the paint with the other. Use an up-and-down tapping motion to apply the paint to the cutout area. Work from the edges toward the center to avoid seepage. You want to get a clean, sharp image.

6. Carefully remove the stencil paper from the wall to reveal the finished design. Reposition the stencil and continue to apply more paint. If the design is to overlap or if you are using more than one color, wait for the first application to dry before continuing.

Wallpapering

Do-it-yourself wallpapering is easy if you start with the right tools. Choose a prepasted wallpaper if you've never done this before. If the room has been previously wallpapered, you'll need to remove the old paper before repapering. If you're hanging paper on damaged walls, you should first repair the damaged areas. If you're hanging paper on new wallboards, coat with latex primer first, so the paper will adhere better.

I've hung a lot of wallpaper on raw walls, over other paper, and over ugly paneling with equal success. I always use prepasted paper. Most papers today are prepasted, except unusual papers that are very costly.

When using this type of paper you have to seal the walls first to prevent paste from being absorbed into them and to provide a smooth surface for the wallpaper. The least costly sealer is glue called wallpaper sizing. It's available in paint departments along with the other tools and materials. You apply this with a roller just as you would paint the walls. This is easy and quick since neatness isn't a factor. Before hanging any wallpaper, paint all your baseboards and window and door trim.

Tools for Hanging Wallpaper

You'll need the following tools, all available in paint stores and home centers, to do a perfect job:

- Metal straightedge at least a yard long for measuring and for long, straight cuts
- Scissors or a utility knife
- Trimming knife and extra single-edge razor blades (replacement blades for the knife)
- Plumb bob or level (use either tool for marking a perfectly vertical line on the wall before hanging the wallpaper strips)

- Paste bucket and paste brush, unless you're using prepasted wallpaper

- Water box, which is made of plastic and looks like a long, shallow feed trough

- Sponge and bucket for clean rinsing water

- Rigid putty knife

- Smoothing brush with ¾-inch bristles for vinyl paper, or a brush with 2-inch bristles for more pliable paper

- Seam roller for smoothing seams and edges

How to Hang Wallpaper

Where you begin or hang the first strip is crucial because this is also where you will hang the last strip. The last strip will inevitably have to be trimmed lengthwise to match the edge of the first strip. Therefore, it's a good idea to begin in a corner or by a door or window where the mismatch won't be too noticeable. If you're hanging paper with a faux finish background such as sponging, the mismatch will be imperceptible.

To Begin

The first strip you hang is the most important because it establishes the pattern for every strip that follows. In other words, if the first strip isn't hung absolutely vertically, all the other strips will be on an angle as well. And the problem gets worse as you proceed around the room. No house has truly vertical walls, so it's best to start in one corner and use a plumb bob to mark a straight line.

1. Begin by measuring the width of a roll of wall covering at the starting point. Subtract about ½ inch and mark your plumb line in one of the following ways:

Rub colored chalk on a plumb bob string and, with a push pin, attach the string to a point high on the wall. Wait until it stops swinging, then pull the bob slightly downward to make the string taut. Press it against the wall and snap the string to leave a lightly colored vertical chalk line on the wall. Or . . .

Hold a carpenter's level against the wall until the upper and lower vials read level. Then, using a pencil, draw a light line down one side of the level. The first strip of paper will go to the left of this line.

2. Measure and cut a strip of paper several inches longer than the height of the wall. Cut the first two strips so the pattern matches. It might be necessary to alternate between two rolls of paper to do this with the least amount of waste.

3. Cover the floor area below where you'll hang the first strip. Fill the water box halfway and place it on the floor where you will begin. Then, starting from the bottom and with the pattern side in, roll up the first strip of prepasted paper. Put it into the water. Hold on to the top of the strip and slowly draw it out of the water, making sure all paste surfaces are wet. It's important to position the edge of this strip along the plumb line, leaving a few inches of paper overlap at the top, rather than trying to line up the top edge with the ceiling or top molding. Smooth the paper onto the wall along the plumb line.

4. Starting at the top center, draw the wallpaper brush down and out to each side edge to smooth and remove air bubbles. Continue to do this all the way down the strip of paper. Use your sponge to remove excess paste as you go along. I often use a putty knife to push the top and bottom edges down and along the baseboard and ceiling molding. Do not trim the excess at this point because when the paper is wet you run the risk of ripping it as you drag the utility knife across it. It's best to wait until the job is finished, or even the next day when it is dry.

5. Line up the next strip against the edge of the first strip so they abut tightly. Use the seam roller to run up and down the seams. With a sponge and clean water, remove excess paste that may come out between the seams.

6. With a pin, release small air bubbles trapped under the paper.

Corners, Windows and Doors

Continue to apply the wallpaper around corners, windows and doors as you come to them.

Corners: Measure from the edge of the last strip to the corner. Cut the next strip 1/2 inch wider. When you hang the second strip, bend the extra 1/2-inch piece around the corner. Make another plumb line on the second wall and hang the first strip so it overlaps this 1/2 inch and extends 1/2 inch around the corner. Use your straightedge and razor blade to cut through both thicknesses in the corner. Peel away the top strip, then lift the edge of the paper and peel away the inner layer. Run the seam roller over the new seam.

Windows and Doors: Let the wallpaper strip overlap the casing of the window or door and, using your putty knife or straightedge, press it into the vertical edge, making a crease. Cut along this creased edge with a razor blade. Crease and cut the paper at the top of the door molding and at the top and bottom of the window areas in the same way.

Carpets

Buying Carpeting

Traffic

For high-traffic areas like dining rooms and living areas, look for a carpet with stain-resistant fibers. Where foot traffic is heaviest, like stairways and hallways, choose a dense, durable pile that can take a beating. In children's rooms, look for a carpet that is easy to clean and tough. At the same time it should be something that kids will want to get down and play on. A pattern to hide soiling is a good idea also.

For low-traffic areas such as dens and living areas that don't get much wear, choose deep pile and luxurious carpets. For bedrooms, think about how you want a carpet to feel when you walk around barefoot.

Estimating cost

To figure out how much carpeting you need, multiply the length of your room by the width in feet and divide by 9. This will give you the square yardage. For example, if a room is 18 x 20 feet, or 360 square feet, divide by 9 to equal 40 square yards. A carpet at twenty dollars a square yard would cost eight hundred dollars. When you buy the carpet, the installer will measure the room to confirm the amount of carpeting you will need.

Carpet Fibers

Wool has a natural luster. It is inherently stain and dirt resistant. It takes dye colors beautifully, and it is extremely durable. It feels good, looks good and is a natural fiber. Too bad it costs so much. Wool carpeting can cost two to three times more than other carpet fibers. If cost isn't the main concern, look at wool carpeting and compare it to the synthetics to see if it is worth the difference in price to you.

Nylon is the most popular carpet fiber in use today. It is durable (more so than other synthetics), resilient and reasonably priced. It works well in a variety of styles and situations and comes in a wide variety of colors. There are many brand names for nylon, and it is universally available. The carpet label will provide information about its stain-resistant features, which are usually familiar brand names such as Stainmaster, Scotchgard, Stainblocker, Wear-Dated, etc.

Olefin is the fiber usually selected for outdoor carpeting, basements and other areas requiring a really durable surface that can be easily cleaned. Olefin is moisture resistant, mildew resistant, weather resistant and colorfast. Astroturf is made of olefin.

Polyester is somewhat softer than nylon but not quite as durable. It is good for low-traffic areas. It is usually less expensive than nylon.

Acrylic is similar to wool in many ways, and is used more in commercial installations than at home. It is generally higher priced than nylon.

Density

The deeper and denser the pile, the better. Closely packed pile that is tightly bound to the backing indicates a quality carpet that will last. You can get an idea of the density of a carpet by folding it over as it would be on the edge of a stair; if you can see the backing, the carpet is not good quality.

Styles and Texture

Carpets are constructed in different ways to create different effects. Almost any pattern or texture can be created using one or another style. There are different degrees of resistance to wear, depending on whether

Tip
When you see a carpet that you like, check the label. There's a lot of information there that can help in making a decision. Also take down the I.D. number so you can find it again.

the carpet is level-cut pile, cut loops, multilevel loops or something else. See below for comparisons. The most important thing is to choose the look of the surface that appeals to you.

Common Styles and Textures

Saxony Plush: This dense level-cut pile of $\frac{1}{2}$ inch or less is closely packed and presents a smooth, luxurious surface. Saxony is frequently used in more formal rooms.

Textured Plush: The tufts are twisted so that the surface has the kind of texture that tends to mask marks such as footprints. For less formal areas.

Frieze: The tufts are twisted or curled in such a way that the surface of the pile is very resistant to wear. Good for high-traffic areas.

Cut Loop: This pattern of high-cut tufts and lower loops has a textured plush that masks footprints. It is generally used in casual areas such as a family room.

Level Loop: The pile is made from loops of the same length. It can take hard wear and is easy to clean, making it popular in informal areas such as children's bedrooms or areas that have high traffic.

Multilevel Loop: This is a looped pile carpet with two or three different heights and loop sizes forming a sculptured surface. These carpets can have a wide variety of "looks." Berber style is typical of multilevel-loop pile.

Random Shear: This features a mixture of cut and uncut loops, creating a highly textured surface appearance. Suitable for both formal and informal settings.

Padding

Your retailer will probably suggest you buy good padding to go under your carpet. This is good advice. The padding can help make the carpet last longer, look better longer and definitely feel better. Padding comes in urethane, flat rubber, rippled rubber and felt. The thing to look for in padding is density (not thickness). Have them recommend the best padding for the type of carpet and the traffic it will get.

Sisal

The look of sisal, flat, warm, natural and unobtrusive, is very popular with designers and homeowners alike. Real sisal (pronounced SIZE-al) is woven from a natural plant fiber. Coir (KOY-er) is very much like sisal and is woven from coconut fiber husks. It is less expensive than sisal. Sea-grass matting, another natural woven fiber, is softer and has a greenish tonality. Sisal has a crisp texture that is very attractive; however, it also is rough to the touch underfoot. Carpet manufacturers produce a myriad of sisal-like carpeting that looks like sisal but is softer, and comes in both wool and synthetic fibers.

Checklist

1. Can you take large samples home to match colors?

2. Does the price of the carpet include padding and installation? If not, how much is each?

3. Check the warranty on the carpet, the padding and the installation.

4. Will the retailer come to the house to measure at no charge?

5. Can you find out where the seams will fall before installation?

6. Are there extra charges for carpeting staircases?

7. Is old rug removal included in the price?

8. Is furniture moving included in the price?

Index

Roman shades, 45, 115, 194
Rubbermaid, 188
rules of thumb:
   for color, 31–32
   for furniture arrangement, 21
   for lamp shade sizes, 79

safety, 151
Saxony plush carpets, 110, 130, 229
Scandinavian Style, 7
Scotchgard, 228
sea-grass matting, 230
seat cushions for sofas, 58
sewing, 13
shades, 97, 156
   Austrian, 45
   balloon, 45, 115
   fabric, 114, 115, 116
   lamp, 79, 143
   matchstick, 45
   roller, 43–44
   Roman, 45, 115, 194
Shaker armchairs, 66
Shaker ladderback chairs, 66
sheets, 127, 133–134, 175
Sheraton side chairs, 67
shower curtains, 175–176
shutters, 44
silk, 40
sisal carpets, 41, 130–131, 230
slat shades, 45
slipcovers, 56
slipper chairs, 63–64
Slumberland, 148
small spaces, 190–195
   accessories for, 194–195
   color in, 190–191
   furniture for, 194
   lighting in, 193
   wallpaper in, 193–194
   walls in, 193–194
   window treatments for, 194
sofas, 54–61
   colors and patterns for, 54–55
   comfort of, 56
   construction of, 61
   depth of, 58
   sectional, 60
   selection of, 55–56, 58, 60
   sleep, 60
   stuffing of, 56–57
   styles of, 57–60
   upholstery fabric for, 54
space:
   closet, 145
   determination of, 21–23
   expanding kitchen counter, 93, 96
   for privacy, 23
   -saving items, 188–189
   small, *see* small spaces
   -stretching techniques for
      bathrooms, 168–170
spattering, 130, 221
sponging, 35, 87, 130, 159, 171, 219
Stainblocker, 228

Stainmaster, 228
stenciling, 36, 42, 87, 130, 154, 158, 221–222
Stewart, Martha, 43, 176
storage:
   in bathrooms, 168–170
   in bedrooms, 145–149
   in children's rooms, 150–151
   in dining rooms, 103, 104, 106
   in home offices, 181–182
   in kitchens, 91
   in living rooms, 76–77
   units for, 84–85, 149
style:
   basics of, 25–26
   definition of, 4–5
   developing personal, 5–6
   evolution in, 29
   flexibility in, 26
   getting started with, 6–8
   online help with, 6–7, 58
Sui, Anna, 176
swags, 111–112, 113
symmetry, 50
synthetic fabrics, 40

tables, 68–74
   all-purpose, 73–74
   alternatives to coffee, 69
   coffee, 68–69
   dining room, 104
   dressing, 140
   end, 68
   height guidelines for, 68
   library, 73
   occasional, 71–72
   occasional drop–leaf, 74
   tea, 68, 69, 70
"tablescapes," 81–82
table setting, 118–119
task lighting, 79
tea tables, 68, 69, 70
tension rods, 47–49
textured plush carpets, 110, 229
Thebes Gallery, 200
Thomas Britt Inc., 204
Thompson's Water Seal stains, 159
3M Company, 154–155
ticking, 40
tiebacks, 112, 113
tiles, 90, 173–174
Today's Homeowner, 6
track lighting, 80
Traditional Home, 120, 205
traffic flow, 18–19
traverse rods, 48–49
trees, 82, 120
trimmings, 134
tulip armchairs, 67

upholstered furniture, 53
   colors and patterns for, 54–55
   fabric for, 54
   see also specific items

valances, scalloped, 114
variations in furniture arrangement, 19–21
Victoria Hagan Interiors, 21
Vogue, 129

wallpaper, 37
   in bathrooms, 173
   in bedrooms, 128–129
   in children's rooms, 155
   around corners, windows **and doors**, 226
   in dining rooms, 108–109
   do-it-yourself, 37, 128–129, **155, 223**–226
   hanging of, 224–226
   in kitchens, 88
   online help with, 31, 218
   in small spaces, 193–194
   tools for hanging, 223–224
walls, 31–40
   in bathrooms, 168, 171, 172–**174**
   in children's rooms, 155
   decoration of, 202–205
   in dining rooms, 108–109
   in small spaces, 193–194
wants, needs vs., 27–28
Wear–Dated carpets, 228
William and Mary armchairs, **66**
window treatments, 43–49
   for bathrooms, 168, 174, 175
   for bedrooms, 131–134
   for children's rooms, 156
   for dining rooms, 110–116
   do-it-yourself, 174, 175
   fabric for, 111
   hardware for, 47–49
   for kitchens, 97
   for small spaces, 194
Windsor armchairs, 67
Windsor side chairs, 66–67
wing chairs, 64
Wolf, Vicente, 64, 172
Woman's Day, 179
Wood, 120
wool, 39, 227–228
World Wide Web:
   www.BHGLive.com, 120
   www.carpetmax.com, 39
   www.domain-home.com, 58
   www.furnituremarket.com, **55**
   www.homearts.com, 7
   www.homecenterweb.com, **166**
   www.homeideas.com, 6
   www.housenet.com, 13
   www.kitchen-bath.com, 88
   www.pdra.org, 31, 218
   www.ncnet.com/ncnw/furn-onl.html, 57
Wright, Frank Lloyd, 66